M000209426

Grace Amazing

STEVE McVEY

HARVEST HOUSE PUBLISHERS

EUGENE, OREGON

Unless otherwise indicated, all Scripture quotations are taken from the New American Standard Bible®, © 1960, 1962, 1963, 1968, 1971, 1972, 1973, 1975, 1977 by The Lockman Foundation. Used by permission. (www.Lockman.org)

Verses marked KJV are taken from the King James Version of the Bible.

Verses marked THE MESSAGE are taken from The Message. Copyright © by Eugene H. Peterson 1993, 1994, 1995, 1996, 2000, 2001, 2002. Used by permission of NavPress Publishing Group.

Verses marked NIV are taken from the HOLY BIBLE, NEW INTERNATIONAL VERSION®. NIV®. Copyright © 1973, 1978, 1984 by the International Bible Society. Used by permission of Zondervan. All rights reserved.

Verses marked ASV are taken from the American Standard Version of the Bible.

Verses marked YOUNG'S are taken from the Young's literal translation of the Bible.

Cover by Left Coast Design, Portland, Oregon

Cover photo © Getty Images / Photodisc Blue / Photodisc Collection

GRACE AMAZING
Previously released as *Grace Land*
Copyright © 2001 by Steve McVey
Published by Harvest House Publishers
Eugene, Oregon 97402
www.harvesthousepublishers.com

Library of Congress Cataloging-in-Publication Data
McVey, Steve, 1954–
   [Living with the King of Kings in— Grace Land]
   Grace amazing / Steve McVey.
      p. cm.
   Originally published: Living with the King of Kings in— Grace land.
   c2001.
   Includes bibliographical references (p.   ).
   ISBN 0-7369-1177-4 (pbk.)
   1. Christian life. 2. Grace (Theology) I. Title.
   BV4501.3.M394   2004
   248.4—dc22   2003021697

All rights reserved. No part of this publication may be reproduced, stored in a retrieval system, or transmitted in any form or by any means—electronic, mechanical, digital, photocopy, recording, or any other—except for brief quotations in printed reviews, without the prior permission of the publisher.

Printed in the United States of America

         04   05   06   07   08   09   10   11 / BP-CF / 10   9   8   7   6   5   4   3   2   1

To my children,
whose love I have never doubted
and for whom my own love will never waver.

Acknowledgments

This book is the product of what God has been doing in my life for the past ten years. After I began to understand my identity in Christ, my pilgrimage from the wilderness of legalism into God's grace-land wasn't an instant event, but a gradual journey. I soon discovered that I had much unlearning to do so that I could progress in grace. Many faithful friends have acted as guides to point me further along the path. I am grateful to my friends in the Association of Exchanged Life Ministries, whose faithfulness in sharing this message helped define my own perspective. Some of what I have written has been the result of what I have learned from these colleagues, who have helped shape my ministry.

I owe a debt of gratitude to a small group of men who I asked to be the first ones to read the manuscript. My desire has been to communicate plain truth in a loving way. These four friends were honest in their critique and will find that numerous suggestions they offered have been incorporated into this book. Special thanks to Bill Gillham, my friend and mentor since my first day on this exciting journey in grace. Much appreciation to my dear friend, Tom Grady, the first one I had ever heard teach the wonderful message of our identity in Christ. Great thanks for the input of Mike Quarles, whose transparent testimony that I first heard in 1990 still impacts my life even today. John Rivenbark, a kindred spirit, spurs me onward deeper into grace every time we are together. These men aren't just friends, but have been pacesetters for my grace walk.

What a joy it is for me to have my friend Gary Smalley write the foreword. God greatly used Gary's books to teach me how to be a husband when I was a newlywed 19-year-old boy who didn't have a clue. For him to write the foreword to this book all these years later is an unexpected blessing that I deeply appreciate. I also appreciate my dear friend Bob Lykens, for being the first one to read the book to edit its grammar so that I would have the courage to allow others to read it. In addition, Bob Hawkins Jr. and the team at Harvest House always work together to produce the highest-quality product possible. I particularly am grateful to my editor for this book. Harvest House has a jewel with Steve Miller, who scrutinized it to make sure the message is presented as clearly and powerfully as possible.

For more than three decades, my greatest encourager has been my precious wife. Melanie knew me when I didn't even know myself and, above any other person, has been the human being through whom Christ has most often spoken to me. In every way, she is the greatest gift from God a man could ever receive for this world.

While deep gratitude is in order for all those mentioned, the praise and glory for it all goes to One alone. This book exists to honor Jesus Christ, whose love and grace is my source and reason for living. Thank You, Lord Jesus, for inviting me to live with You in Your amazing grace. I love it here! Use this book to draw sincere people out of empty religious routine and into the wonderful land of grace where You are everything to us.

Contents

Open Your Heart to God's Grace

Grace Amazing is a book that may change the way you understand the Bible. In fact, it may transform your Christian life!

After reading what Steve McVey says about God's grace, I have come to see Scripture so differently. Now, when I read what appears to be a commandment or direct instructions from God's Word, I no longer feel the pangs of guilt or the sick feeling that comes from trying to live out what I think God wants me to do for Him...and failing. I now read these verses with the freedom and joy of knowing that they can come true in my life by God's grace as His Spirit lives through me.

Grace Amazing reminds us that God's grace applies to every area of our lives, even stubborn habits. We may feel there are certain problems that can't be overcome, but such thinking comes from an incomplete understanding of grace. From the beginning of my Christian life I've understood how God's grace gives us eternal life and forgiveness from sin, but I had either forgotten or become cold in my application of how it works on a personal, everyday basis. I had tried to discipline myself to live the Christian life the right way and do it on my own. *Grace Amazing* reminded me that we're not called to live this life in our own strength, but in Christ's.

How exciting it is to rest in Christ and wait for Him to live within me through His Spirit! How different life is when we leave the path of self-sufficiency and yield to God's grace! His grace works where our strengths and abilities are not sufficient. When we live in His strength, we know true rest—the kind of rest God yearns for every Christian to know.

I thank Steve for writing about God's priceless grace in such a way that hopefully many others will avail themselves of it. As you read, I encourage you to open your heart to the message of *Grace Amazing;* you may find it will transform your Christian walk!

—Gary Smalley

Bestselling author and speaker

one

BECAUSE OF HIS AMAZING GRACE...

Religion Is Now Poison for Us

"I'M SICK AND TIRED OF IT ALL. All this church talk is just religious junk. God knows that I've tried to live the Christian life. I've taught both of my children how to live a Christian life. I've taught them from the time they were babies! Now this happens. I'm sick of it. I have friends who have never even taken their children to church once and they haven't had to face this kind of mess. I've been sincere, but this is all a big joke. It just doesn't work. I know you believe in all of this, Steve, but I don't anymore. The Christian life just doesn't work."

I sat silently while Wayne expressed the rage he felt, which had begun to surface two days earlier when he found out that his youngest daughter was pregnant. He had cried when his daughter told him the news. He had expressed to her his heartfelt grief over the fact that in a moment she had thrown away her youth as well as the infinite possibilities for the future. Then he had wrapped his arms around her and whispered in a breaking voice, "We'll get through this somehow, baby. You're 17 and I'm not going to make you go through this alone." That night he had held his wife, Joan, as she cried herself to sleep. He had said all the right words to his family, but for the past two nights, in the stillness of the early morning hours, he had lain awake with his brain being mercilessly pounded by a single thought: *Where did I fail her? I taught her better than that! She knows how to live a Christian life.* Where did I fail?

What do you tell a man like Wayne? There was a time when I would have given him some pat answers that I heard in seminary or catchy phrases I learned from other pastors who had no idea what he was facing. I don't do that anymore. After 30 years of seeing the empty look that comes into people's eyes when they have religious clichés hurled into their bleeding faces, and after having had life slam me between the eyes with a few hard knocks of my own, I have made the conscious choice to never do that again.

> *Our generation has little tolerance for thoughtless Bible-babble that has no connection to their own lives.*

We are living in a day when rote, religious answers just won't do it for people anymore. They will respond to spiritual reality, but our generation has little tolerance for thoughtless Bible-babble that has no connection to their own lives. People like Wayne have been Romans-eight-twenty-eighted to death.[1] Don't misunderstand me—I firmly believe that people need the eternal truths that are found in the written Word of God. But they won't settle for a glib Bible verse like a child accepts a rabbit foot when told it will bring him good luck.

To be specific, people like Wayne need a Christlike response, not a religious one. What did I tell him? I simply pointed him to the One who understands his confusion and his pain. I made no effort to give him definitive answers about the *why* of his situation. As has often been the case when I talk to people devastated by life's circumstances, I didn't know the reason why. Instead I pointed him to the *Who* of every difficult circumstance we will ever face in life. I've learned over the years that when I don't know what to say about the whys of life, the best thing to do is to point to the Who of all things. Religion tries to systematize everything into neat little compartments that readily offer hollow answers for the unanswerable. Jesus never does that. He simply points to Himself and gently whispers, "Believe."

Allow me to go ahead and set the tone for the remainder of the book: I'm not big on religion; in fact, it leaves a bad taste in my mouth. Maybe it's because I swallowed so much of it for so many years. I was a pastor of local churches for over 20 years. I've served up and eaten every dutiful dish of dead doctrine you can imagine. My problem wasn't a lack of sincerity. To the contrary, I was very sincere. But then so was Paul when he was persecuting the church, all the while thinking he was doing God a big favor. Don't think that I'm saying I have renounced my faith in Jesus Christ. My disdain for religion hasn't diminished my love for Jesus Christ and His church. Rather, the opposite has occurred. Since God's grace has leveled the religious wall which partially obscured my view of Christ, I've come to love Him more deeply and serve Him more fervently than ever before.

Those precious friends in the churches I have served might differ with my assessment of most of my pastoral ministry. It's true that many people did come to know Christ during all those years before I began to understand what it means to live and minister in grace. Many Christians were blessed and hurting people were healed. That fact simply proves the truth of an axiom I heard in seminary: "God can hit a straight lick with a crooked stick." I don't negate the work of God in my life during those days. In His grace, God looked beyond my confused mind and saw a sincere heart. But measurable results can't have the last word on the accuracy of one's message or methods, or else Christ-denying cult groups would be proven more accurate than many Christ-honoring churches.

Poison in the Pot

There is a story in 2 Kings that illustrates the kind of ministry that often exists in modern church life. It's a story about poison being served up by sincere men of God.

> *When Elisha returned to Gilgal, there was a famine in the land. As the sons of the prophets were sitting before him, he said to his servant, "Put on the large pot and boil stew for the sons of the prophets." Then one went out into the field to gather herbs, and found a wild vine and gathered from it his lap full of wild gourds, and came and sliced them into the pot of stew, for they did not know what they were. So they poured it out for the men to eat. And it came about as they were eating of the stew, that they cried out and said, "O man of God, there is death in the pot." And they were unable to eat* (2 Kings 4:38-40).

Gilgal was the home of the renowned "School of the Prophets," founded by the great prophet Elisha. One day Elisha instructed one of the sons of the prophets to prepare a meal. Someone went out into the field and gathered wild gourds from a wild vine and put them in the stew. The prophets poured the stew out for everyone to eat when someone discovered, "There is death in the pot!" God's prophets were serving poison and eating out of the same pot.

That's what I did for many years. I took the liberating gospel of God's grace and mixed the *wild* gourds of religious performance in the same pot with it. The gourds came from a *wild* vine out in the field.[2] Grace doesn't grow in a wild field. It is cultivated only in an infinite garden of love planted and nurtured by God Himself. The idea of religious performance is a wild plant that poisons the grace of God and causes it to cease to be edible, although I did eat and serve it to my churches for many years. The tragedy of this kind of poison is that it won't kill you, but will be just toxic enough to keep you sick for the rest of your life.

The underlying foundation of all religion is *performance*—whether it's a tribal dance around a campfire to satisfy the fire god, or a dead religious activity performed week after week by an evangelical Christian with the intent of impressing his God. It's all religious performance, and God isn't impressed by our performance. What impresses Him is faith. "Without faith it is impossible to please Him" (Hebrews 11:6). He couldn't care less about religious ritual void of life. God is in the business of life. Nothing else interests Him. When it is all said and done, God will either raise dead things or else ultimately separate Himself from them as far as He can get. He is interested in living relationships, not dead religion.

The Wilderness of Religion

The announcement of the gospel of grace includes the good news that God wants to deliver us from religion. He has extended His grace for the purpose of rescuing us from a lifestyle of futile, feeble efforts to make ourselves acceptable to Him. The essence of religion is man's attempt to somehow convince himself that he has jumped through enough hoops for God to give him the approving nod. It's the way we try to validate our own self-worth, but our acts of self-righteousness actually separate us from the very goal we seek to achieve. Religion is poison because it kills any opportunity one will ever have to experience genuine intimacy with God. Religion is a prostitute having sex with a man and telling him it's love, when all the while, deep in his heart, the man knows better. Religion offers the false hope that somehow there is *something* we can do to impress God enough to cause Him to accept us on the basis of our actions. Religion is what rushes in to fill the vacuum created by the absence of personal intimacy with God.

> *G*od is interested in living relationships,
> not dead religion.

In reality, when a person doesn't experience intimacy with God through Jesus Christ and attempts to approach God through his religious acts, his deeds will be an affront to the perfectly righteous God who demands nothing less than perfection. Since none of us can possibly walk perfectly, we might as well stay off that road altogether.

Yet many believers, who by divine sovereignty have been brought out of Egypt and miraculously placed on The King's Highway, have now filled their tank with the gasoline of religion and their engine with the oil of self-effort and think they are on their way to the land of victorious living. They are often making good speed, but what they don't know is that they are driving in circles. They are pleased with their performance, but don't know they are going nowhere fast.

The story of Israel's journey through the wilderness illustrates well the life of the Christian who is trying to achieve spiritual success through religious performance. God delivered the Jewish people from Egypt so that they could be led into the promised land of Canaan, and they are a picture of what God desires to do in the lives of those who trust Him. He wants to bring us from the bondage of an empty life into the land of amazing grace—a place where He showers us with good things for no other reason than because He loves us.

As Christians, there's nothing for us to do to deserve entry into this wonderful land of grace. Like Israel, we have been miraculously led out of our past slavery so that we can immediately take possession. We only need to walk into the land that is ours—without delay and without any cost or obligation on our part.

The land of Canaan was where Israel was to become a great people who would be blessed by God and who would themselves be a blessing to others. It is often described in Scripture as a land flowing with milk and honey, a description that denotes a place where not only would their needs be met (milk), but they would also enjoy the sweet abundance (honey) that God planned to give them. God wanted to take the Israelites to this special place and pamper them with His goodness and generosity. Notice that God never gives the bare minimum; He generously *lavishes* gifts on those He loves. This new land would be a place where Israel would live in paradise, with God making everyone's lives more wonderful than they could ever imagine. Theirs would be an abundant life like they had never experienced before, and it would be in a land of rest.

However, the people couldn't accept God's promise at face value. It was too easy. "Surely we must do our part," they may have reasoned. Doing our part—that's the toxic element in religion. Religion is an insidious virus that infects the Christian and ruins what would otherwise be a clean bill of health. We simply can't believe that God expects *nothing* of us after He delivers us from the sins of our own Egyptian bondage. Surely we must owe Him *something* despite the fact that any attempt to place a price on a priceless gift is to disparage its value. To enter a life of victory without any effort on our part? That's too simplistic. So it was with Israel: "And so we see that they were not able to enter because of unbelief" (Hebrews 3:19).

Why would I suggest that Israel's life in the wilderness can serve as a picture of the lifestyle of believers whose lives are characterized by religious performance? There are at least two similarities between Israel and religious performers that are too glaring to ignore.

Both are characterized by a struggle to experience victory. The people of Israel knew what it was to struggle. They had spent 400 years enslaved in Egypt, serving cruel taskmasters who showed no mercy. Then they wandered in the wilderness for four decades, struggling to enter the place God had promised to Abraham. I'm sure that oftentimes this promise seemed like no more than a spiritual story taken from the past, which had little relevance to the daily struggles in their lives. Their actions often revealed their belief that somehow their own efforts were integral to entering into the promised land.

Their feelings weren't unlike the feelings of those today who desire to experience the victorious life that is promised in the Bible. They sincerely try to attain this life through religious efforts, but a successful, consistent walk with Christ seems to elude them constantly. No matter how hard they try, there is always a vast wilderness between where they are and where they want to be.

Both are characterized by repeated rededication to try harder. The biography of Israel in the wilderness shows a 40-year pattern of trying, failing, and rededicating themselves to try again. The people sincerely wanted to enter into Canaan, but all the sincerity they could muster never could bring them into the land. Their life story is marked by short-lived moments of victory, followed by a decline in faith that led to failure, then a renewed commitment to try again. Sound familiar?

An Invitation to Canaan

Joshua must have become scared when he was told that he would be the man who would lead the children of Israel into Canaan. After all, there were two-and-a-half million of them and they had acted like fussy, spoiled children during most of their travels in the wilderness. Yet if the story of Israel's wandering in the wilderness and their entry into the promised land demonstrates anything, it shows how persistent God is in bringing about the good that He has promised to those who belong to Him. If God didn't lovingly and patiently continue to work with His immature children, we all would have been in trouble long ago.

Are you hungry for a more satisfying reality in your spiritual life? God loves you too much to leave you in a tawdry affair with religion. He wants you completely for Himself. You can file this away as an unalterable fact: God isn't going to give up on you. There's nothing you can ever do that will cause Him to shrug His shoulders and walk away. Nothing. By divine determination, His invisible hand will relentlessly guide your steps until He brings you to the place where He can do for you everything He wants to accomplish.

God wants to bring you out of the barren wilderness of religious performance and into the fullness of a life in grace. His intention from the beginning has been that you should *enjoy* your faith relationship with Him. He wants you to live in

Canaan—the land of amazing grace, where the most important thing is that you and He revel in the love that you share together.

Having served as a local church pastor for many years and having been a Christian since I was a young child, I know both by observation and experience the agony of substituting religious

> *God loves you too much to leave you in a tawdry affair with religion. He wants you completely for Himself.*

activity for spiritual intimacy with Jesus Christ. It is possible to do all the right things outwardly and still miss the inner peace and joy that come only from our union with Him. God doesn't want those He delivers from sin to get stuck in the wilderness of lifeless religious activity. He wants us to move into the enjoyment of His grace, knowing that when we experience our true life in Him, our activity will be animated by a divine power and accompanied by a personal satisfaction that can come only from Him.

Break Off Your Affair with Religion

"Steve, I'm glad I was finally caught. You can't imagine how exhausting it is to be involved in an affair! It is physically, mentally, emotionally, and even spiritually draining in a way that I can't describe. I'm glad it's over." I could tell that Rob was sincere. His yearlong affair with a lady at work had recently been discovered by his wife. Although it was obvious that their marriage would require a long period of healing, it appeared that they were going to survive adultery.

Exhausting—that was the word Rob used to describe his affair. It's a good word to describe the lifestyle of one who is married to Jesus Christ and yet having an affair with religion too. An adulterous affair poisons a marriage. It takes one's time, energy, interest, and love from the one who should be the recipient of all these things and pulls them into a ruthless vortex of destruction, which isn't satisfied until every good thing meant to be known in marriage is destroyed.

That's what religion does in the life of the believer. Multitudes of Christians have abandoned the intimate, loving relationship they once enjoyed with Jesus Christ and have settled for a sleazy affair with religion. There was a time when they reveled in the union they share with Him, but gradually they took their eyes off Christ and began to focus on their own religious performance. They have, as Jesus once said to a church in Asia Minor, "lost [their] first love."[3]

If you can identify with those whose love for Christ has grown cold and who now try to find spiritual fulfillment in religious activity, I lovingly implore you: Break off the relationship you have with religion and return to your first love! Does it sound harsh that I should begin this book by saying that religion is poison? My only purpose in using harsh analogies and pointed remarks as we move together through this book is to sound the alarm in the church. Many of us have been seduced and deceived. We have been seduced by religion and deceived into thinking that as long as we *do* the right things, everything is okay spiritually. We've been enticed into an adulterous relationship with another lover, and an ugly one at that. Michael Yaconelli has rightly asked,

> What happened to radical Christianity, the un-nice brand of Christianity that turned the world upside down? What happened to the category-smashing, life-threatening, anti-institutional gospel that spread through the first century like wildfire and was considered (by those in power) *dangerous?* What happened to the kind of Christians whose hearts were on fire, who had no fear, who spoke the truth no matter what the consequence, who made the world uncomfortable, who were willing to follow Jesus wherever He went? What happened to the kind of Christians who were filled with passion and gratitude, and who every day were unable to get over the grace of God?[4]

It is my hope that as we move through the chapters of this book together, your heart will be opened and your mind will be renewed to *that* kind of Christian lifestyle. It's not about religion. It's only Jesus. *Jesus.* He's all that really matters.

Let's walk together with Israel on their journey from the wilderness into Canaan. You may find that there are some paths along the way that you would rather not walk upon because they are unfamiliar. You might find a few thorns along the journey that prick your traditions and cause you to feel uncomfortable. You might even be tempted to put down the book and abandon the trip.

However, I encourage you to travel the distance with me. I may challenge your thinking in ways that make you feel uncomfortable at times along our journey, but I promise you one thing: I will always point you to Jesus Christ at every juncture along the journey. I will never intentionally encourage you to take one single step on this pilgrimage that isn't charted in God's unchanging Word. The Bible will be our map, and Jesus our destination.

Do you want to live enjoying God's amazing grace? Then let's possess the land. However, I must warn you: First, it will be necessary for us to pass together through some deep waters.

Walking Together

Let's walk together with the Holy Spirit through this book. As God reveals truth to you, it will be helpful to cooperate with Him at each step where He works in your life. If the prayers at the end of each chapter express your heart, then affirm to God that they reflect your thoughts and desires. You will get more out of this book if you pause at the end of each chapter and interact with your heavenly Father.

Dear Father,

I recognize that at times I have been more focused on religious duties than on You. I want more than to be religious in my lifestyle. What I do want is to experience Your life in me each day. Give me an open mind and heart, and help me discover the truths You want me to learn from this book.

G.R.A.C.E. Group Questions

A G.R.A.C.E. (Giving & Receiving Affirmative Christian Encouragement) Group is any group of people who gather together to encourage and strengthen each other in the grace of God. At the end of each chapter are questions to help facilitate further learning and discussion. The truths of this book will be worked further into your life as you consider these questions.

1. Read 2 Kings 4:38-40. What are some of the poisonous beliefs you've had in your life that have interfered with your ability to live a victorious Christian life?

2. Religion stresses a form of behavior without the presence of divine life. What are some common ways modern churches tend to be more religious than spiritual?

3. This chapter describes two ways that the wilderness could be compared to empty religion. Name two other similarities.

4. List three ways that Christians often try to find fulfillment through religious activities instead of from Jesus Christ.

5. Discuss the ways that the land of Canaan is a spiritual picture of the Christian life.

$\mathcal{G}$od Will Put More on You Than You Can Bear

I HAD KNOWN ED JACKSON for many years. All of his adult life he had been successful in business. Coming straight out of college, where he had been an admired running back on the football team, he moved immediately into a career position that would take most men ten years to attain. Ed soon married his college sweetheart, Julie, a beautiful lady, and before long they had two picture-perfect children. He was the kind of man many would envy. He was living the American dream—he had a successful career accompanied by an affluent lifestyle, a beautiful wife, and two exceptional children. It seemed that everything in life was being handed to him on a silver platter.

One day when Ed returned to the office after being out of town for a few days, he found a piece of paper on his desk that simply read, "Ed, see me. Kent." Ed strolled into Kent's office without a clue that another piece of paper awaited him there. It was a memorandum telling him that his job would end in 30 days. Kent explained something about a new C.E.O. who wanted to bring in his own team. Ed remembers the pained expression on Kent's face when Kent had broken the bad news to him. Kent wasn't only his immediate supervisor, he had become a friend.

Three weeks later Ed and I sat in a restaurant together as he expressed his pain. "It makes no sense at all. This is one situation I can't solve. I'm in too deep. My life is out of control!" At the time, I didn't think that he was looking for answers. Sometimes people just want to vent their pain and frustration to a friend without having the friend immediately try to fix them and their problem. I sensed this was one of those moments. I responded only with sincere sadness and compassion, trying to communicate my love and concern for him and his family.

Problems may be our personal escort to lead us straight into the place God has prepared for us.

In the weeks that followed I shared with Ed some biblical truths that applied to his situation. Several times he said to me, "I'm in this too deep. My life is totally out of control!" Finally the time came when I felt it was appropriate for me to speak the truth in love.

"Yes, Ed. You *are* in deep water here, but you aren't going to drown. Your life isn't out of control. It's simply out of *your* control."

"It's a spiritual attack from the devil!" he quickly countered.

"I would encourage you not to be so quick to give the enemy the glory for your troubles," I answered. "This may be the hand of God working in your life to accomplish His goal for you."

It is easy to blame our troubles on the enemy when we can make no sense of our circumstances. However, in doing so we make a mistake by failing to recognize that troubles may be the hand of God at work in our lives. The greatest opportunities for us to advance spiritually are often couched in adversity. Problems may be our personal escort to lead us straight into the place God has prepared for us.

Facing Deep Waters

Like Ed, Joshua knew about deep waters. He must have awakened in the early morning hours on the day he was to lead Israel across the Jordan River and into Canaan. His heart probably raced as he thought about the prospect of moving two-and-a-half million people across the flooding river. This would surely be a miraculous day that the people would remember forever, if they didn't drown.

Between the place where Israel stood in the wilderness and the promised land was the Jordan. Running a distance of 70 miles from the southern tip of the Sea of Galilee to the northern end of the Dead Sea, the river is normally about ten feet deep at its deepest points and about a hundred feet wide. The elevation of the river drops from around 700 feet below sea level at the Sea of Galilee to almost 1300 feet below sea level where it ends at the Dead Sea. The word *Jordan* means "the descender." The biggest problem that Israel would face trying to walk across was the swift currents caused by the descending geography of the valley.[1] At some places the water in the Jordan River runs downhill *fast*. In fact, there are 27 series of rapids along its route down to the Dead Sea.

When the day came for the Israelites to cross over, the people had spent three days camped on its banks, watching its swift current. They knew the power of the river's strong current under *normal* conditions would make it difficult to walk across, but conditions weren't normal at this point. It was harvest season, and "the Jordan overflows all its banks all the days of harvest"

(Joshua 3:15). God didn't choose for the people to cross the Jordan River into Canaan when it would be difficult. He waited until it would be *impossible* for them to do it themselves.

Ed and Joshua lived millennia apart, but they shared a similar problem. They both faced circumstances that were impossible to find a way through without a miracle. Impossible situations—those are the kind that God likes to create for those who follow Him. It is only when a believer has come to the end of confidence in his own ability to navigate his way that he will enter into the land where God's grace dwells. God doesn't just *allow* us to face impossible situations. As the Sovereign of every circumstance, He often *designs* such situations in order to bring us to the end of our own self-sufficiency.

The culture in which we live values self-sufficiency, in fact, it often *honors* it. Yet God places no value on our self-sufficiency at all. His thoughts and ways are not ours. He wants to bring us to the place where we realize that we cannot experience successful living on our own. He wants us to see that we can't accomplish a victorious life, but rather must accept it entirely as a gift. However, coming to the place where we give up on our own self-sufficiency doesn't come easily for most of us. God can place the gift of victory into only an open hand, not one clenched tightly around one's own assets. Often the only way He can bring us to the place where we can receive is to send a flood into our lives. Only when we are in too deep to handle life ourselves are we more likely to abandon ourselves completely into His loving hands.

God Won't Let You Succeed

Many Christians believe that if they are sincere enough and try hard enough, they can successfully live a godly lifestyle. Yet God wants us to realize that no matter how long and how hard we try, we will never be able to successfully live as a Christian. God doesn't intend for the Christian life to be hard to live; He intends for victorious living to be *impossible* for us to achieve on our own. Only He can do it through us, and He will do whatever is necessary to bring us to the place where we see that.

I remember seeing something on television long ago that illustrates how we often try to manage our own lives. Did you ever see *The Ed Sullivan Show?* Even if you aren't old enough to have watched Ed Sullivan when he was on television, you probably have seen this act in reruns. There was a man who would spin plates on the top of long rods that measured about ten feet in length. He would start by spinning one plate on a rod, then he would stand the rod straight up with the plate still spinning on top, high up in the air. He would then gently shake the rod in such a way as to keep the plate spinning on top.

He would then take another rod and plate and do exactly the same thing again. Then he would take another…and another… and another. Eventually the man would have about a dozen plates spinning in the air all at the same time. Then he would frantically run back and forth across the stage, shaking the rods and keeping the plates going. He could keep all of them going at the same time. It was amazing to watch.

That man's act reminds me of a Christian who is enslaved to living in the wilderness of empty religion. Religion demands that we keep all our plates in the air. The plates represent the things of value from our own religious perspective—things that we believe *we* must sustain. The religious legalist spends his whole life running back and forth, "shaking his sticks" in an effort to manage his life. Surely none would argue that *this* is the life Christ died to give us! What a waste His death would have been.

Meanwhile, our loving heavenly Father sees us wearing ourselves out with this performance we call "the Christian life."

Moved by compassion, He determines to deliver us from the frenzied routine we have mistakenly thought of as "Christian living." So He walks across the stage of life and starts knocking our plates off the rods. One by one He causes them to fall and shatter at our feet.

It's interesting to see how the body of Christ reacts to this plate-breaking movement of God. I'll bet you never read about *that* movement of God in Christian magazines. How would you like "The Breaking Revival" to come to your church? People's lives would all start falling apart so that Christ could become their sufficiency.

To try is nothing more than religious performance, and God loves us enough that He will spoil our performance if necessary.

Different parts of the body of Christ respond to God's breaking process in different ways. The Baptists conclude that they need to rededicate themselves to try harder to keep their plates in the air the next time. The Pentecostals begin to rebuke the demon of plate-breaking. The charismatics lay hands on the plate and say, "In Jesus' name, be healed!" The Presbyterians conclude that the plate must have been predestined to break from the foundation of the world. The Methodists form a committee for a yearlong study on the causes of the plate-breaking and to determine whether it was a sin for the plate to break or simply the inherent predisposition present in the plate since the day of creation. The Salvation Army responds, "When you think about it, aren't we *all* really broken plates?"

In writing this, it isn't my goal to offend Christians of every denomination. I hope you have a sense of humor and can see that what I want to point out is that while different parts of the body of Christ respond to our problems in different ways, we all have the same tendency. We fail to see that God may be the One who is causing our problems to come so that He can bring us to the place where we give up on our self-sufficiency and begin to totally trust in Him alone.

God wants to bring each of His children to brokenness, a condition that exists when we have given up all confidence in our own ability to manage life. Before we can cross over into His land of grace, we must come to the end of ourselves and recognize that we will never accomplish victory by our own strength. To *try* is nothing more than a religious performance, and God loves us enough that He will spoil our performance if necessary.

When Israel prepared to cross over into Canaan, the people had no doubt that it would take a miracle for them to get across the Jordan. The flood-stage waters preached a sermon to them: "You can't do it because it is impossible. Only God can." Once they said "Amen" to that truth, they were ready to go across, but not a minute sooner. The same acknowledgment is necessary on our part before we can enter. We must come to the point where we realize that it isn't hard for us to live a victorious life; it is *impossible* for us to do it. Only one Person can live the Christ-life, and that is the Christ Himself. He will live it through us only when we give up on our own efforts and learn to abide in Him.

Burdens Greater Than We Can Bear

The title of this chapter is intended to shake you up in order to wake you up. Maybe you have heard all of your life that God won't put more on you than you can bear. I don't believe it.

God *will* put greater burdens on you than you can bear. In response, perhaps your mind is racing to 1 Corinthians 10:13: "No temptation has overtaken you but such as is common to man; and God is faithful, who will not allow you to be tempted beyond what you are able; but with the temptation will provide the way of escape also, that you may be able to endure it." While it's a good verse, it doesn't disprove my assertion that God *will* put greater burdens on you than you can bear. First Corinthians 10:13 is talking about temptation to sin, not burdens. It's true that God will not allow you to be tested beyond your ability to endure, but the same can't be said about the troubles He allows in your life.

Consider the words of the apostle Paul in 2 Corinthians 1:8-9:

> *We do not want you to be unaware, brethren, of our afflic-*
> *tion which came to us in Asia, that we were burdened*
> *excessively, beyond our strength, so that we despaired even*
> *of life; indeed, we had the sentence of death within ourselves*
> *in order that we should not trust in ourselves, but in God*
> *who raises the dead.*

Let's dissect those two verses and determine exactly what they mean in light of the burdens that we experience as Christians.

- *Paul's trouble seemed to come from nowhere.* Paul said that he didn't want the Corinthians to be ignorant about the trouble that *came to him* while he was in Asia. Have you ever felt like you were walking through life minding your own business when suddenly here comes trouble? Seemingly out of nowhere, we are sometimes ambushed by problems.

- *Paul's burden was excessive.* Paul contends that not only did he find himself facing a burden, but it was an excessive one. It was trouble to an extreme degree.

- *The burden was beyond Paul's strength.* There is the biblical proof—he said the problem was "beyond our strength" (NASB). Other translations read that Paul said his problem was "far beyond our ability to endure" (NIV); "beyond our power" (ASV); "above our power" (YOUNG'S). It doesn't take a Bible scholar to see what Scripture clearly says in this text. Just look at the plain words of Scripture. Paul's burden was more than he could bear.

- *The burden caused Paul to despair of life.* Lest anyone argue with the weight of what he has already said, Paul states that he despaired of living. Death would have been a welcomed release (compare with Philippians 1:23-24).

- *Paul's problem was a death sentence to him.* The burden Paul carried caused him to feel like the kiss of death was on his circumstances. Have you ever felt like everything you did faltered and died right before your eyes? Paul knew what it was to feel that way.

As a young man I found myself at a place in ministry where I sometimes wished I could die. I served as a local pastor in a hard place where it seemed that circumstances continually progressed from bad to worse. There were critics in the church who often drove me to the point of despair. One of the leaders of the church actually asked me one day, "How do you really *know* that there is a God?" While serving there my income was repeatedly reduced until I could barely eke out an existence for my family. Get the picture? That church wasn't exactly a Disneyland for pastors who served there. Certainly there were some loving people there who remain friends to this day, but overall it was a very hard place to be.

My response to the situation was not unlike that of many pastors in similar circumstances. I went to the printer and had a thousand résumés printed, and began circulating them to everybody I knew and to some people I *didn't* know. I wanted to go to a new place. I reasoned that if God would only put me in the right kind of situation, things would be better. Eventually I became bitter and rebellious toward the Lord in my heart. I went through the motions of ministry, but my heart was turned away from God. I was angry because He wouldn't help me by changing my circumstances. I was burdened excessively, beyond my strength, so that I despaired of life. I had the sentence of death on myself.

"In Order That We Should Not Trust in Ourselves"

Can you relate to the confusion and anger I felt? I'm certainly not attempting to justify my feelings or actions at the time. I'm simply being honest with you about where I was in my life at that point in time. Have you ever faced circumstances that caused you to feel the way I have described?

I wish that when I faced those difficult days I had understood the truth that sustained Paul when he was overtaken by his burden. A question many people often ask when facing tough circumstances that cause them to feel forsaken by God is, "Why?" Why would God allow Paul to face such extreme burdens that he despaired of life? Why would He allow a zealous young pastor to be overwhelmed by adversity until he was crushed by the weight of his problems?

The Bible gives a clear and concise answer to the question. Second Corinthians 1:9 says this happens "in order that we should not trust in ourselves, but in God who raises the dead." Trust in ourselves is the default setting of contemporary society. It is applauded in American culture as a virtue, but God's perspective stands in sharp contradiction to the opinion of man. He loathes our independence, instead desiring that we become like little children who recognize our need to totally depend upon

Him. While society may be attracted to strength, God is repulsed by human self-sufficiency. The thing that He finds most attractive in man is weakness and the realization of the need to be completely sustained by Him alone.

Michael Yaconelli tells the story of a woman who was on vacation on one of the barrier islands in South Carolina. It happened to be the time of year when the loggerhead turtles (huge 300-pound sea turtles) were laying their eggs. One night the woman discovered a loggerhead laying her eggs. Not wanting to disturb the turtle, she decided to come back the next morning to the place where the turtle had laid her eggs. When she returned the next day, she was alarmed to find the turtle's tracks were headed in the wrong direction, away from the sea. The turtle had apparently lost her bearings and wandered into the hot sand dunes, where she would surely die.

The woman followed the tracks and soon found the turtle covered with hot, dry sand. She quickly poured cool seawater on the turtle, covered her with seaweed, and went for help. She returned shortly with a park ranger, who flipped the turtle over, wrapped tire chains around her front legs, and hooked the chains to the trailer hitch on the Jeep. He then drove toward the sea, dragging her through the sand, filling her mouth with sand and bending her head back as if it would break. Reaching the beach, he unhooked her and flipped her right side up. As the waves washed over her, she began to move slowly, then pushed off into the water and disappeared. The woman later observed, "Watching her swim slowly away and remembering her nightmare ride through the dunes, I noticed that sometimes it is hard to tell whether you are being killed or saved by the hands that turn your life upside down."[2]

Sometimes we may feel as if God is dragging us through the sand. We may wonder why He permits us to be hurt. We want to be strong, but we find ourselves in circumstances that continue to weaken us more and more. As a result, we become discouraged and want to give up, which is actually a good thing. God finds a weak person to be irresistible. He says, "To this one I will look, to him who is humble and contrite of spirit" (Isaiah 66:2). The Lord "saves those who are crushed in spirit" (Psalm 34:18). He is opposed to those who are strong. It is those who have been humbled who receive His grace (James 4:6). Our résumé may impress the people around us, but God is impressed only by those who know they are complete losers apart from His intervening grace. We don't get strong enough to be useful to God; we must become *weak* enough (see 1 Corinthians 1:26-29).

Consequently, when God prepares to use a person's life for His glory, that person must be totally stripped of self-sufficiency. God won't be anybody's co-pilot. He doesn't even simply want to be the pilot. He wants us to know that He is the pilot, the airplane, the runway, the air that holds us up, and the final destination at which we will arrive. In other words, He is everything. He is our very Life. "In Him we live and move and exist" (Acts 17:28).

This Can Be Your Liberation Day

Is your goal in life to become a victorious Christian? The only way that will ever happen is if you admit that you can never accomplish it. You can only *receive* it. Israel wandered in the wilderness of self-sufficiency for 40 years. Some Christians have lived there that long too. It's easy to be self-sufficient in a religious lifestyle, but to walk in grace requires that we voluntarily give up control of our own lives. In order to motivate you toward that end, God may lead you to the place where a rushing flood is before you.

God uses the floods of life to bring us to the place of absolute surrender to Him. Are you tired of living like you've been living?

I have discovered in my own life that doing all the right things isn't enough. Religious behavior is the way many try to control their lives and, in a sense, control God. Our approach to the Christian life is as absurd as the enthusiastic young man who had just received his plumber's license and was taken to see Niagara Falls. He studied it for a minute and then said, "I think I can fix this."[3] We may reason that if we *do* the right things God will be pleased and bless us, but God doesn't care about what we do unless it is an expression of the union life we share with Him.

God finds a weak person irresistible.
He "saves those who are crushed in spirit."

My friend Ed Jackson, who came home from vacation to find that he had lost his job, eventually came to understand this truth, and it set him free from the fear that initially gripped him. One day I asked him, "Ed, are you willing to give up the control of your own life and surrender yourself and every part of your existence into the hands of God?"

Tears filled his eyes and he nodded. We bowed our heads and he began to pray, "Lord, I know that I'll never enter into the lifestyle You have for me until I'm willing to let go of control over my own life. By faith I choose to do that very thing at this very moment. In Jesus' name, amen."

That day was Ed's Liberation Day. It is the day he crossed the river.

Are you willing to relinquish control over your own life? The only way we will enter into enjoying God's amazing grace is to live in total abandonment to Him. Total abandon means that we willingly surrender the deed to life into His hands. It is an intentional yielding of every detail of our existence to His control, trusting Him to do whatever He may want to do in us, to us, or through us. It is a leap of faith that takes us from our own pathetic attempts to create security and into the hands of a sovereign God.

Absolute surrender to God is scary to the extent that we don't know or trust His character. Yet God will often allow us to face circumstances that thrust burdens upon us that are greater than we can bear so that we will be motivated to trust Him and take our hands off our own lives. It is a step of faith taken in spite of the fact that we may feel fearful and be uncertain of the future.

Many Christians have already trusted God to lead them out of the bondage of the past. They have trusted Him to forgive their sins, but then have taken the control of their lives back into their own hands. They are sincerely *trying* to find their way into Canaan, but their efforts have led them to endless wandering in a religious wilderness.

Many of us are tired of religion. Deep in our hearts, we know there *must* be more to being a Christian than what we have experienced. There is. Yet to experience more than empty religious ritual, it is necessary that we abandon ourselves to Him and begin to move forward in faith.

Israel may have stared at the swift waters of the flooded Jordan River and concluded, "Yes, the water is deep and the current is swift. Common sense indicates that we could be swept away if we step into the water to cross over, but *we are tired of living like we've been living.* We're willing to risk it all in order to trust God. We will follow Him and whatever happens, happens."

Are you ready to cross over? Then step into the water by abandoning yourself and everything you think you've ever known to Christ. Then prepare to move forward into a new land. Leave all your religious baggage behind. You won't need it where you're going. You will soon discover that God's land of grace is unlike any place you have ever been.

Dear Father,

I now realize that the need in my spiritual life is not to be stronger, but to be weaker. I have often tried to swim through the deep waters of life by myself. When there have been times I couldn't get myself through, I have chosen to tread water until things got better. Teach me to trust You and to know that Your main goal isn't to change my circumstances, but to free me from self-sufficiency. I now abandon myself into Your hands. I trust You.

G.R.A.C.E. Group Questions

1. Describe the most recent circumstance in which God allowed you to face deep waters.

2. Read 2 Corinthians 1:8-9. Why will God allow a Christian to be burdened beyond his own strength? Why does God value weakness in people and not strength?

3. Define the meaning of absolute surrender to God. Why are Christians sometimes afraid of absolutely surrendering everything in their lives to God?

4. Recount a time when a friend shared a problem with you. What did you tell him? Would your answer to him be different now? Why or why not?

5. Define *brokenness*. Are brokenness and suffering the same thing? Can one experience suffering without experiencing brokenness?

three

Much of What We Thought We Knew Is Wrong

"I CAN'T LIVE THE CHRISTIAN LIFE!" Gene seemed passionate, almost angry, when he made this statement to me one day.

"What is the Christian life?" I asked him.

"You know what the Christian life is, Steve," he answered with mild irritation. "It is doing what Jesus would do in every situation. It's having Him as number one in my life. But there's no way that I can understand how to make that happen, considering what it's like to work in my company. And we won't even talk about my marriage. I ask myself every day how He can be number one in a relationship where two people hardly seem to even notice each other anymore. I don't know what He would do if He were married to my wife! I honestly pray every day, but nothing changes."

As I continued to talk with Gene, it became apparent that he had the same problem that many other people have. He was convinced that he had accurately diagnosed his problem and that he knew the correct answer. He sincerely believed that his assessment of the situation was based on absolute, unquestionable truth. He needed to "do what Jesus would do" in every situation and "have Him as number one" in his life. I decided to go ahead and intentionally say something that I knew would shock him so I could get his attention.

"Gene, I want to propose an idea to you that you might think is radical, but that I believe is biblical."

"What's that?" he said.

"You've been trying to make Jesus number one in your life, right?"

"Yes," he replied.

"Well, I don't believe He *wants* to be number one in your life. In fact, I think your attempts to make Him number one by doing what He would do are a big part of what's causing your problems."

"What are you talking about?" he asked, uncertain of where I was going.

I continued, "What if much of what you've learned about living as a Christian is wrong? What if there is a way of life for the Christian that is different than anything you've known?" I could tell by his expression he was skeptical and defensive, yet curious.

You've Never Known Life Like This

Israel was about to be led into a new life, one that would be completely different from anything they had ever known. Joshua gave the orders to his officers and they conveyed them to the people: "When you see the ark of the covenant of the LORD your God with the Levitical priests carrying it, then you shall set out from your place to go after it" (Joshua 3:3). Then he told them plainly, "You have not passed this way before" (3:4).

You have not passed this way before. This is one of the great understatements of the Bible. God's people were about to enter a dimension of living so unlike anything they had ever known that they couldn't even imagine what the new world would be like. So it is with the Christian today who moves from the wilderness of religious legalism into the land of grace. To live there is to experience the reality of who we are in Christ. To compare the difference between living a religious lifestyle and experiencing a grace walk is to compare two dimensions of living that are more diametrically opposed than a person can conceive until he has crossed over from one to the other.

In 1990 the Lord began to teach me my identity in Christ and since then I have lived in a different world.[1] The new world of grace causes wilderness living to pale to rubbish by comparison. Max, a photographer, described his own experience well when he told me, "Before I knew my identity in Christ, my life was like a 3 x 5 black-and-white still photograph, but when I came to understand what it means to experience Him living through me, my life became like a full-length motion picture with all the special effects!"

Consider the questions I posed to Gene in response to his effort to make Jesus number one in his life. What if much of what *you* have learned about living as a Christian is wrong? What if there is a way of life for the Christian that is different than anything you've known?

Just Because We Haven't Heard It Doesn't Mean It Isn't True

I believe two things are very important as we travel together through this journey. First, it is important not to be gullible. It is a sad fact that there is much false teaching in our day that attempts to pass as spiritual truth. As Christians we have a responsibility to measure what we hear by the Bible before we assimilate it into our belief system. Paul said of the Berean Christians, "Now these were more noble-minded than those in Thessalonica, for they received the word with great eagerness, *examining the Scriptures daily, to see whether these things were so*" (Acts 17:11, emphasis added). It is important to determine whether or not concepts that are new to us can stand up to the scrutiny of God's Word.

Yet there is another side to this coin, especially when it comes to the matter of grace in the lives of Christians. This is the side of the issue that has paralyzed many believers, keeping them from moving forward in spiritual growth. It concerns our willingness to accept biblical truth that may be new to us. Having acknowledged the importance of not being gullible, look to the other side of the coin and consider this question: *Are you teachable?* Just because a truth may be new to you doesn't mean that it is a new truth. No truth is really new, only newly realized.

What if there is a way of life for the Christian that is different than anything you've known?

Many Christians have systematized their spiritual beliefs into orderly compartments that they feel are neatly arranged and easily managed. Anytime they hear something that is new to them, they attempt to fit it into one of those self-designed compartments. If it won't fit, they reject the new concept without giving it any further consideration.

This fact presents a real problem when it comes to the matter of moving people from the wilderness of religion into God's grace-land. Why? Because there is no place where legalistic religion and grace can intersect. Law and grace can never coexist together; consequently, a Christian whose lifestyle is primarily religious in essence may have great difficulty crossing over into the new land. One must move *out* of the wilderness in order to move *into* Canaan. To accept grace means to renounce legalism—a system of living in which we try to make spiritual progress or gain God's blessings based on what we do. That kind of paradigm shift can sometimes come with great resistance after one has lived in the wilderness for a long time.

> Whenever someone attempts to introduce a radically different insight to people whose minds have been formed by an old and well-worked-out way of thinking, he or she is up against an obstacle. Jesus said their taste for the old wine is so well established that they invariably prefer it to the new. More than that, the new wine, still fermenting, seems to them so obviously and dangerously full of power that they will not even consider putting it into their old and fragile wineskins. But now try to see the point of the biblical imagery of wine-making a little more abstractly. The new insight is always at odds with the old way of looking at things. Even if the teacher's audience were to try earnestly to take it in, the only intellectual devices they would have to pick it up with are the categories of the old system with which it conflicts. Hence the teacher's problem: if he leaves in his teaching a single significant scrap of the old system, they, by their very effort to understand, will go to that scrap rather than to the point he is making and, having done that, will understand the new only insofar as it can be made to agree with the old—which is, not at all.[2]

Robert Capon pinpoints the problem, saying, "We grant you that the theology of grace has suffered gross neglect—that we have reached a point at which almost all people, inside the church as well as outside, find that the notion of grace stands in contradiction to everything they understand by religion."[3]

Genuine Truth Is Grounded in God's Reality

Having been born into a world system in which every religion known to man stresses his responsibility to stay in favor with his god through specifically defined behavior, it requires a radical paradigm shift for most Christians to move into a mind-set that embraces the idea that our behavior has absolutely nothing to do with gaining or *staying in* God's favor. To suggest that there is nothing the believer can do that would put him out of favor with God sounds almost blasphemous to the religious mind. Most of us who grew up in church *know better* than that, don't we? Therein lies the problem. Often as much must be *unlearned* as is learned about walking in grace as a believer. Theologian Krister Stendahl astutely observed that "it is not so much what we don't know, but what we think we know that obstructs our vision."[4]

One significant barrier that prevents many people in the modern church from enjoying a life in grace is what they *think* they know. They are firmly entrenched in a paradigm of spiritual reality that to them is self-evident, however imaginary it may actually be. Without divine intervention, the religionist will never experience grace to its fullest extent. Recipients of grace must have a heart and mind that are open toward God, and nothing so decidedly shuts down one's capacity to receive as empty religion.

Let's go back to my conversation with Gene. His belief that Christ should be number one in his life is more than truth to him. His idea that he should attempt to do what Jesus would do in any given situation is a spiritual *reality* to him. While one's viewpoint on truth may be examined, or even questioned, *reality* is never questioned because nobody ever even considers that it *can* be questioned. On his own, Gene would never consider that his opinion might be out of line with reality. His viewpoint is a *self-evident* truth to him—a reality.

Gene is experiencing what Charles Kraft calls "subjective reality." Kraft contends that there is both an objective REALITY and a subjective reality. We look at an eternal REALITY and take a kind of photograph of it with our minds. Then we operate on the basis of that mental picture. Thus the REALITY "out there" is mediated to our minds through a mental picture that we ourselves construct.[5]

Is Our Reality Also God's Reality?

Many believers think they understand the truth about grace yet have never even begun to comprehend the REALITY of its beauty in full bloom. Would you be willing to consider for a moment that some of the ideas about the Christian life that you have held as truth may not be grounded in REALITY? As we move forward in a growing understanding of God's grace, we will begin to see that the grace of God is so much bigger and better than we had imagined.

To gain an expanded understanding and appreciation of the grace of God, we must be willing to admit that we may not have everything correctly sorted out in our belief system at the present moment. An unwillingness to have our mind changed will imprison us in the wilderness; it will keep us from fully enjoying all that God so longs for us to have.

I heard a story about a man who was fishing one day when another man sat down a few feet away and watched him. He noticed that, contrary to what fishermen usually do, the man would keep the small fish and throw the big ones back into the water. Finally, the observer's curiosity got the better of him.

"Sir, I can't help but wonder: Why are you throwing back the *big* fish?"

"Because my frying pan is not big enough to cook them," the fisherman answered.

That's what has happened to many in the modern church: Their "frying pan" is simply too small to contain the larger truths of God's grace. As Charles Kraft points out:

> While we have seen the "big R" REALITY, we perceive it as "small r" reality. Our perception is always subjective, focused, limited, and partial. Though we cannot understand absolutely, we need to learn as much as possible about REALITY and to adjust our perception of reality accordingly. To do this we must learn to be open to understandings that lie beyond those we now have. We need to keep searching for new insights in REALITY and adjusting our perceptions to those new insights. This involves constant comparison between our present views and those we become aware of through other people and new experiences, including books.[6]

These adjustments in our beliefs must be governed by the Bible and not by any religious indoctrination we may have received. It is important to recognize that the two are not always synonymous. Don't confuse the "small r" religious teaching that you may have received with the "big R" REALITY of the Word of God. While the Bible is totally trustworthy, anything we may have been taught is fair game for critical scrutiny, which ultimately may lead us to reject the teaching in question if it doesn't align with the Bible.

In a lively discussion among friends, one man was asked, "What do *you* believe?"

"I believe what my church believes," he responded.

"What does your church believe?" he was asked.

"My church believes what I believe," he calmly responded.

"Well, what do you *both* believe?" he was challenged.

Without hesitation, the man answered, "We both believe the same thing."

Such blindness caused by religion will be a lifelong malady unless the Great Physician intervenes.

Recipients of grace must have a heart and mind open toward God, and nothing so decidedly shuts down one's capacity to receive as empty religion.

An essential element in whether or not one will be able to experience the joys of living in God's new land rests in how open he is to growing in grace. People like Gene are so mired in the muck of religious misinformation that they must have divine intervention if their minds, and consequently their lives, are to ever be rescued by the unconditional, limitless grace of God. I have skirted all around the question that must be answered. Now I put it to you bluntly: Are you willing to have your mind changed about some of the things you have always believed?

I was discussing a theological issue with a friend one day and said to him, "I just finished reading a book on this subject that blew my mind. I became so frustrated at some points of the book that I wanted to put it down without finishing it."

"Why?" my friend asked. "Was it because the author's arguments suggested that you have been wrong in what you have believed about the subject?"

"No," I answered. "It's worse than that. He *proved* it!"

It's never comfortable to have our doctrinal idols destroyed. The degree of difficulty in having our opinion on a subject changed is in direct proportion to how intricately embedded the belief is in our minds and lives. Some people don't want to be confused with the truth, but to move into grace-land it is necessary to leave on this side of the Jordan River those worn-out religious folk tales which, until now, we have always cherished as sound doctrine.

Christ Doesn't Want to Be Number One in Your Life

I have chosen two popular religious untruths to illustrate how vehemently one may hold to his perception of reality, despite its underlying fantasy. First, consider Gene's belief that he must make Jesus number one in his life. His goal sounds admirable, and at first glance biblically sound, but there is a subtle danger in his perspective. It presupposes that Christ *wants* to be number one in our lives. Why would that perspective present a subtle danger? Allow me to answer that question with a question that I hope makes the answer obvious.

If Jesus Christ wants to be number one in your life, who holds second place? For the Christian there is no number two. Jesus Christ will not be denigrated by being on anybody's list. He *is* the whole list because He is our whole Life. For the Christian there is no life apart from Jesus. For us to live *is* Christ (see Acts 17:28; Philippians 1:21; Colossians 3:4). Jesus didn't come to take a place in our lives, even first place. He came to become our Life. He is number one, number two, and number three. He's the whole list, the source of everything.

Every new Christian understands the all-pervasive place of Christ. Nobody has to tell him that Jesus is to be number one in his family, on his job, or in his leisure life. Nothing of the sort would even occur to him. Christ as number one? His understanding is that Christ is *everything*. The newly born Christian is consumed with Jesus Christ. Then at some point he is ambushed by religion, with all its rules about how to make Jesus be number one, and the rest, as they say, is history.

Andrew Murray comments:

> When first the believer finds Christ as his righteousness, he has such joy in the new-made discovery that the study of holiness hardly has a place. But as he grows, the desire for holiness makes itself felt, and he seeks to know what provision his God has made for supplying that need. A superficial acquaintance with God's plan leads to the view that while justification is God's work, by faith in Christ, sanctification is our work, to be performed under the influence of the gratitude we feel for the deliverance we have experienced, and by the aid of the Holy Spirit. Often the believer struggles hopelessly for years, until he listens to the teaching of the Spirit, as He glorifies Christ again, and reveals Christ, our sanctification, to be appropriated by faith alone.[7]

Our flesh so wants to *do something* to contribute to our holiness. When Gene was told plainly that he didn't need to try to make Christ number one in his life, it didn't set well with him. He was at a critical juncture in his Christian walk at this point. He could embrace the truth that Jesus Christ *is* his life, rest in that truth, and thus be liberated from the tyranny of trying to make

Him be what He in REALITY already is. Or he could clench his religious fist around his "small r" reality that he must try to make Jesus be number one and stumble away into the darkness of legalistic demands that will forever refuse to be satisfied.

Have you chosen a rest or a list? Jesus said, "Come to Me, all who are weary and heavy-laden, and I will give you rest" (Matthew 11:28). The invitation is to leave the wilderness of religion and come on over to the land of God's grace, where you don't have to struggle anymore. When Jesus ascended back to the right hand of the Father, He sat down for a reason. The job has been done. Believers have been justified, sanctified, and glorified (see Romans 8:29). There's nothing left for us to do except believe it, relax, and enjoy the journey. If there were anything left to do to put God and the Christian in a right standing with each other, Jesus would have done it. The fact is that He *did* do it—all of it.

> *Jesus didn't come to take a place in our lives, even first place. He came to be our Life.*

After writing seven chapters championing the complete sufficiency of Christ's work on the cross, the writer of Hebrews says, "Now the main point in what has been said is this: we have such a high priest, who has taken His seat at the right hand of the throne of the Majesty in the heavens" (Hebrews 8:1). The struggle for our holiness is over and Jesus has sat down to prove it. Gene had always believed that he must work hard to make Christ first in his life. He was wrong. Christ *is* his life. Have you been wrong about that too?

The Belief That We Must Do
What Jesus Would Do Is Wrong

Gene also believed that he was supposed to do what Jesus would do in every situation, another fallacy that has found renewed popularity in our day. Charles Sheldon's classic work, *In His Steps,* and the acclaimed work of Thomas à Kempis, *Of the Imitation of Christ,* have both fostered the idea that the Christian's behavior should be rooted in the question "What would Jesus do?" While there is good in both of these books, it is unfortunate that they encourage a lifestyle of imitation.

There is no way that a believer can successfully imitate the life of Jesus Christ. Even a cursory reading of the New Testament reveals a holiness of life that is absolutely beyond our reach, barring a miracle of epic proportions. Consider this short list of a few basic things the Bible says Christians are to do if we are to be like Jesus:[8]

- We are to walk as Jesus walked (1 John 2:6).
- We are to love our enemies (Matthew 5:44).
- We are to forgive as Jesus forgave (Colossians 3:13).
- We are to be kind to those who hate us and even pray for them (Matthew 5:44).
- We are to consistently be overcomers—more than conquerors (Romans 8:37).
- We are to give thanks in every situation of life (Ephesians 5:20).
- We are to never worry about anything, but always have peace (Philippians 4:6).
- We are to rejoice in the Lord always (Philippians 4:4).
- We are to be holy (1 Peter 1:16).
- We are to stand out in bold contrast to this wicked world (Philippians 2:15).

- We are to hate ourselves and renounce our selfish desires daily (Matthew 16:24).
- We are to keep our focus on heavenly things (Colossians 3:1).

Have you had enough yet? These are only a dozen ways that we are to be like Christ. He did every one of these things constantly and perfectly. How have you done with these twelve? Can you consistently do ten out of twelve? Six of the twelve? Even one of the twelve? If we aren't perfectly and consistently doing them all, it's a pathetic joke to think that we can imitate the life of Jesus Christ. Even if you could perfect these twelve, I must inform you there are hundreds more where these came from. Don't think that all God expects is your best effort either, because the Bible makes it very clear that God doesn't grade on the curve.

The belief that the Christian life is an imitation of the life of Christ is *wrong*. Any Christian would tell an unbeliever that he can't become a Christian by looking to Jesus as a model of behavior. Every Christian knows that salvation requires that one receive the life of Christ by faith. Why then do so many people, having become Christians, now think that the life of Jesus becomes a model for them to imitate? Jesus Christ has placed His life into us so that He can live His life through us. It has nothing to do with imitation but everything to do with participation. "For we have become *partakers* of Christ" (Hebrews 3:14, emphasis added).

Leaving Our Wrong Theology in the Wilderness

I spent the first 29 years of my Christian life committed to some beliefs that I sincerely thought were truth but eventually came to see were wrong. I don't need to make Jesus Christ number one in my life. He *is* my Life! I don't have to ask the question, "What would Jesus do?" He lives inside me and will express His life *through* me if I'll only trust Him to do it. The WWJD (What Would Jesus Do?) bracelets and bumper stickers that are so popular today point in the wrong direction. One friend said that the letters should represent "Watch What Jesus Does!" As believers, we have the Spirit of Jesus Christ dwelling within us (see 1 Corinthians 3:16). As we trust Him, we participate in the expression of His divine life through us. To attempt to imitate Him is a cheap substitute for authentic Christian living.

As the Israelites prepared to cross over the Jordan River into Canaan, Joshua's words may have echoed in their heads: "You have not passed this way before." Leaving behind the wilderness of religion brings much more than subtle cultural differences. It is REALITY because God's grace-land is His hometown. It is moving into a land where much of what we knew to be true before has no significance anymore. It's the start of a new life with a new identity, a place where everything we have been and known before is *cut away* in a way that is astounding.

Dear Father,

I realize how presumptuous I have been at times in thinking that I have the "right" understanding of everything I believe. I don't want to be gullible, but I do want to be teachable. Please enable me to receive truth from You that may be new to me. Keep me from rejecting an idea just because I haven't seen it that way before. Enable me to examine what I read in the light of Your Word to see if it's true. If it is, then grant me the humility to have my mind changed.

G.R.A.C.E. Group Questions

1. Name one area of your beliefs where you have experienced a radical change from what you used to believe.

2. Read Acts 17:11. What should be the response of the Christian when confronted with ideas that are new to him?

3. This chapter suggests that Jesus Christ doesn't want to be number one in your life. Discuss both sides of this statement, giving the pros and cons of each side. What do you believe? Why?

4. List three problems with asking ourselves the question "What would Jesus do?" What would be a better question for the Christian to ask? What is the difference between imitating the life of Christ and participating in His life?

5. What are some obstacles that prevent people from changing their opinion about something they have long believed?

four

BECAUSE OF HIS AMAZING GRACE...

$\mathcal{O}$ur Old
Sin Nature
Is Dead

I WAS TEACHING ON THE SUBJECT of our new identity in Christ when Dirk began to squirm in his seat and laugh out loud. He was seated about five rows from the front. I tried to ignore him and keep on teaching, but he became more and more expressive and vocal about what he was feeling. Finally, I walked over to the side of the platform near where he was seated and said, "You look like you're having a good time. What's going on with you?"

"I just realized something," he answered. "I was an alcoholic *in another life!*" Immediately I knew what he meant. Dirk had just realized the truth that when we enter the land of God's grace, we receive a brand-new identity and leave the old one behind. He had been an alcoholic before he met Christ, but at salvation his old identity had been cut away and he had received a brand-new identity.

It was the first day in the new land when the Lord spoke to Joshua and said, "Make for yourself flint knives and circumcise again the sons of Israel the second time" (Joshua 5:2). It had been 40 years since any man in Israel had been circumcised. This was a serious matter, considering the meaning that circumcision always had among the Jewish people. Circumcision had been the sign of God's covenant with His people. He had first spoken of circumcision and His covenant to Abraham when He said, "You shall be circumcised in the flesh of your foreskin; and it shall be the sign of the covenant between Me and you" (Genesis 17:11). A circumcised Jew was a Jew who acknowledged faith in his covenant God. In the New Testament, Israel is sometimes referred to as those "of the circumcision." From the time of God's command to Abraham, the men of Israel had always been circumcised. Yet the whole time that Israel had wandered in the wilderness, none of the men had been circumcised. They were still God's covenant people, but they hadn't been acting like who they were.

Knowing Who We Used to Be

Before a person is a Christian, he has one nature. It is the sin nature, which he inherited by being in the family of Adam. When Adam sinned in the garden of Eden, he died to God and suddenly found that it was his nature to sin. In an instant, all of mankind became dead to God because of the choice made by Adam. "Through one man sin entered into the world, and death through sin, and so death spread to all men, because all sinned" (Romans 5:12). We were all born spiritually dead because when Adam died spiritually in the garden, we were *in* him. Consequently, whatever was true of him became true of us. "By the transgression of the one the many died" (Romans 5:15). Every person born into this world has a sin nature because we are born into the family of Adam.

Ephesians 2:3 says that before we became Christians, we "lived in the lusts of our flesh, indulging the desires of the flesh and of the mind, and *were by nature* children of wrath, even as the rest" (emphasis added). A man flatters himself who believes that before he becomes a Christian he isn't all *that* bad. In reality, however, his very nature is an offense to God. The Bible teaches that until one is born again he is ungodly (Romans 5:6), a sinner

(Romans 5:8,19), an enemy of God (Romans 5:10), spiritually dead (Romans 5:12), and condemned (Romans 5:18). Before salvation, every person "walked according to the course of this world, according to the prince of the power of the air, of the spirit that is now working in the sons of disobedience" (Ephesians 2:2). An unbeliever who believes he is good errs by comparing himself with other people instead of seeing the perfectly righteous character of God. If we compare rotting corpses, it makes little difference whether the body has been dead for a week or a month. The relevant fact is that the man is *dead*. All unbelievers are spiritually dead and fall short of God's standard of righteousness (see Romans 3:23). It is a person's very *nature* to sin when he comes into this world. Nobody has to be taught how to sin. The Bible teaches that the wicked go astray from the womb. They are born speaking lies (see Psalm 58:3).

When we enter the land of God's grace, we receive a brand-new identity and leave the old one behind.

I remember the first time I ever saw this truth illustrated in a way that makes it evident that we are all born with a sin nature. It was about six weeks after we brought our first-born child home from the hospital. We were playing with him in the living room and he was in a wonderful mood. He laughed and smiled, obviously enjoying his parents' attention. After a while, it was time to put him to bed. "What do you think about letting him sleep in the crib in his own room tonight?" Melanie asked me. Until now, he had always slept in our bedroom with us.

"I think it might be a good idea," I answered. So we both went into his bedroom and Melanie gently laid him down in the baby bed. She leaned over and kissed him on the cheek, then I did the same. He softly cooed and smiled at us as we turned to leave the room. *What an angel!* I was thinking.

We both went back into the living room and had just sat down on the couch when we heard a bloodcurdling scream come from his room. *Oh, no!* I thought. *He must have pulled himself up and fallen out of the bed!* Melanie and I jumped to our feet. It was obvious— our precious little six-week-old boy was in serious trouble. *Maybe he has his head caught between the bars of the bed and is choking!* I agonized as we rushed to his room. *I hope he's not bleeding!*

As we burst into the room, we both rushed over to his bed and looked down at him. He instantly stopped crying, looked up at us, smiled, and with a gentle voice, said, "Ah-h-h-h." "He just wants to be picked up," Melanie said.

"What a little liar!" I laughed. "He screamed like he was hurt just so we would run in here and pick him up."

You might argue that a six-week-old baby couldn't devise such a sinister strategy, and I agree. I don't seriously believe that he sinned that day. I'm simply making a point: Nobody has to be taught to do wrong. We have reared four children, and they each mastered the skill of lying at one time or another. I never taught them that. Even though I jokingly told their mother that they took after her side of the family, in reality, it was an intrinsic ability they received from Adam (through me). Just like me, my children were born knowing how to sin because they were born with a sin nature.

Man's Greatest Need Is Not to Stop Sinning

The citizens of this earth sin because it is their nature to do so. Only those whose "citizenship is in heaven" have the ability to consistently say no to sin. Many well-meaning Christians in the modern church seem to have embraced the goal to curb sin on planet earth, an objective akin to trying to mop up the incoming tide on the beach. If all Christians could band together and force everybody else to stop sinning and begin to live by Judeo-Christian values, what spiritual difference would it make? From an eternal perspective, it would make absolutely none. People would still have the same problem. They would be left *in Adam* and therefore still be sinners.

Watchman Nee once asked a class of children, "Who is a sinner?" and their immediate reply was, "One who sins." He responded,

> Yes, one who sins is a sinner, but the fact that he sins is merely the evidence that he is already a sinner; it is not the cause. One who sins is a sinner, but it is equally true that one who does not sin, if he is of Adam's race, is a sinner too, and in need of redemption. Do you follow me? There are bad sinners and good sinners, there are moral sinners and there are corrupt sinners, but they are all alike sinners.[1]

Were it possible to stop a person from sinning, his moral improvement would be inconsequential because he would still be a sinner. Consider Dirk, who was addicted to alcohol before he became a believer. What if a well-meaning Christian had made it his project to see Dirk freed from addiction to alcohol? There are many methods that could have been used to accomplish the goal. Some of them might even have been successful, but where would that have left Dirk? If the only thing accomplished was that he lived in freedom from his addiction, Dirk would have still had the same basic problem. His problem wasn't that he was addicted to alcohol; that was only a symptom. His problem was that he was spiritually dead. He was a child of Adam, ruled by a sin nature that opposed God at every point.

What Dirk needed wasn't new behavior. He needed the new birth! He needed to have his old sin nature, which loved to be drunk, be forever removed from him. Dirk needed far more than rehabilitation; he needed resurrection. He didn't need to learn how to *deny* his desire to get drunk, but instead needed to be *delivered* from the desire to get drunk. He needed a *new identity.* That kind of transaction would require a miracle, but miracles are no problem for God.

The Circumcision of Our Old Nature

God's covenant sign under the old covenant of Law was circumcision. Why would He choose such a thing as a sign of the covenant He has with His people? It is because of what it depicts. He wanted the circumcision of Israel's men to be an object lesson pointing toward what would happen to His children under the new covenant of grace. Physical circumcision is the cutting away of a piece of skin on a man's body at the place from which life originates, and by which his gender (part of his identity) is identified. When the skin is cut away, it never grows back.

The apostle Paul points out that in this day of grace we have been circumcised "with a circumcision made without hands, in the removal of the body of the flesh by the circumcision of Christ" (Colossians 2:11). At salvation, God reached down and cut away from you the source of your old life. That source was the sin nature with which you were born because you inherited it from Adam. When you became a Christian, God removed it from you and it will never grow back.

The Jews on the banks of the Jordan used flint knives to circumcise their males, but God's instrument for our spiritual circumcision was the cross. The cross is the focal point of the Christian faith because every good thing that God has done for us and in us originates at the cross. At the cross God placed us into Jesus Christ and the source of our old life died. The old sin nature we had before becoming Christians was cut away forever. This is an objective truth we must embrace if we are to enjoy living in God's grace. The old person we were is dead!

Consider the following verses, noting the emphatic teaching that our old nature died:

> *Knowing this, that our old self was crucified with Him, that our body of sin might be done away with, that we should no longer be slaves to sin* (Romans 6:6).

Our old man is the old Adamic nature that characterizes everybody who is born into this world. This old sin nature was crucified so that we would no longer be slaves to sin.

> *For you have died and your life is hidden with Christ in God* (Colossians 3:3).

What died? It was our old sin nature, who we used to be. If you struggle with this fact, then the question must be addressed: "If it wasn't our old sin nature that died, what *did* die?" It wasn't our body or our soul. It was the sin-filled spirit that Paul calls "our old man." Our sin nature is dead.

> *I have been crucified with Christ; and it is no longer I who live, but Christ lives in me; and the life which I now live in the flesh I live by faith in the Son of God, who loved me, and delivered Himself up for me* (Galatians 2:20).

Andrew Murray remarks on this verse:

> How blessed must be the experience of such a union with the Lord Jesus! To be able to look upon His death as

mine, just as really as it was His—upon His perfect obedience to God, His victory over sin, and complete deliverance from its power, as mine; and to realize that the power of that death does by faith work daily with a Divine energy in mortifying the flesh, and renewing the whole life into the perfect conformity to the resurrection life of Jesus![2]

How wonderful it is to know that the old person we were before salvation died with Christ! The Bible repeatedly asserts this truth (see Romans 6:2-3,7-8,11; 7:6; Galatians 2:19; Colossians 2:20; 2 Timothy 2:11). I offer an abundance of verses because it is important that you be convinced of the death of your old sin nature. If the thought of your old sin nature being dead is contradictory to your feelings, your understanding of your own experiences, or the church tradition in which you may have learned otherwise, I challenge you to *examine the Bible* and allow Scripture to be your final authority. Choose to believe what God says regardless of what you may be inclined to think or feel.

It Takes Time to Heal After Circumcision

Although our old nature has been cut away, that doesn't mean that all the residual effect of our old life is instantly gone. After the Jews entered Canaan and were circumcised, it took time for them to heal. The Bible doesn't say how long that time was, but remember that they were circumcised with a sharp *rock* (we're talking serious commitment here!). We can be certain that healing didn't happen overnight.

Don't assume that because your old nature has been put to death everything that fueled your lifestyle in the wilderness will instantly disappear. Although your spirit is now filled with the life of Jesus Christ, the *soul* must be gradually renewed, and that takes time. The soul is our personality, consisting of our mind, will, and emotions. Part of the ongoing sanctification process that the Holy Spirit does in our lives is to bring healing to our damaged emotions and to renew our minds to the truth of God's Word. Living in the land of God's grace is not a lifestyle of sinless perfection; rather, it is a place in which God can gradually bring about the healing that we may need in our feelings and beliefs.

"Why don't I have the confidence I need to really influence other people's lives for Christ?" Annette had been to my office for counsel many times over the past few months. I knew her history of abuse as a child, both mentally and sexually. She had been molested by both her uncle and her next-door neighbor. When she told her mother about the neighbor, her mom's response was, "Just stay away from him." Concerning her dad's brother, her mother's answer was, "Your dad would kill him if he found out what he did, so don't mention this. Just don't get too close to your uncle." So Annette did exactly what her mother told her to do—she withdrew. Except she didn't withdraw from only her uncle and her neighbor; she pretty much withdrew from everybody. She learned to be an introverted child whose basic desire was to be invisible to those around her.

In her thirties, Annette came to understand her identity in Christ. She made the move into the new land, but she still struggled with *feelings* of insecurity. Her mind knew better, but her feelings told her that she would be hurt if she became too close to people. In the weeks that followed, I showed Annette what the Bible says about walking in faith. I explained that faith is simply a confidence in God and that her need wasn't to have greater *self-*confidence, but to express greater confidence in Christ and His ability to express His life through her. "You mean that I should simply *act* like it's not me who is interacting with other people, but that it is *Jesus* who is relating to them?" she asked one day. "That's a pretty good way to describe it," I answered. "You simply need to trust Him to be your Confidence in every situation."

Some time after that I saw Annette at church one day. She walked over to me smiling, leaned over, and whispered, "I had to go to a social function for my husband's company last night. I *felt* nervous, but you should have seen Jesus there. He did a good job!" I understood. Annette is choosing to let Jesus *be* Jesus in her and she is waiting for her feelings to change in His time. Feelings may not change instantly when we enter the land, but we often find

At the cross God placed us into Jesus Christ and the source of our old life died. The old sin nature we had before becoming Christians was cut away forever.

ourselves rising above our ability and living out of a Life-Source greater than ourselves. There *is* healing when we come into the promised land. It just doesn't always happen immediately. You can believe that your old nature is dead and gone and *act* in faith, knowing that God will guide you continually and will gradually bring healing to your feelings and thought processes.

Freedom from Our Past

All Christians know that when we enter into Jesus Christ we receive a new future. Our eternal destination becomes heaven, not because of what we do or don't do, but because we are now *in Christ.* Yet what many believers don't know is that we also have a new past. Because we are a new creature in Him (see 2 Corinthians

5:17), His past becomes our past. The person who was in Adam is dead. We are not simply changed at salvation; we are made somebody *new*. To say that one becomes a different person when he becomes a Christian doesn't mean that he has been simply changed. It means that his old life has been *exchanged* for a new one—the very Life of Jesus Christ Himself!

One of the great benefits Israel enjoyed when she entered Canaan was having the shame of her past removed. "Then the LORD said to Joshua, 'Today I have rolled away the reproach of Egypt from you.' So the name of that place is called Gilgal to this day" (Joshua 5:9). Nothing so handicaps a man in his walk with God as trying to drag around an old shameful identity. Who you *were* and who you *are* have no connection anymore. In Jesus Christ, we don't only have a new future, we have a new *past!* The person you are now has been "in Him before the foundation of the world" (Ephesians 1:4). The person you *were* is dead. The new you has a past that is blameless and spotless.

Consider Dirk, who laughed out loud and said, "I just realized something. I was an alcoholic *in another life*." He didn't mean that he had been reincarnated. Dirk was understanding for the first time that while he had been an alcoholic before he became a Christian, that man is dead now. In his new life in Christ, he has a new identity. His past life has been totally removed from him. Paul describes this miraculous transaction in 1 Corinthians 6:9-11:

> *Or do you not know that the unrighteous shall not inherit the kingdom of God? Do not be deceived; neither fornicators, nor idolaters, nor adulterers, nor effeminate, nor homosexuals, nor thieves, nor the covetous, nor drunkards, nor revilers, nor swindlers, shall inherit the kingdom of God. And* such were some of you; *but you were*

washed, but you were sanctified, but you were justified in the name of the Lord Jesus Christ, and in the Spirit of our God (emphasis added).

Drunkards (or alcoholics) don't go to heaven. But Dirk is no longer an alcoholic. He has been washed, sanctified, and justified! Dirk the drunkard is dead. Can a saved man *act* like an alcoholic? Of course. Yet it is important to know that who we are and how we act don't always coincide. Melanie sometimes tells me when I am sick that I'm a big baby, but it's not true. I have a birth certificate to prove it. Actions don't determine our identity—birth does.

When we entered into Jesus Christ, the shame of our old life was rolled away. We may still behave in certain wrong ways when we try to get our needs met apart from Christ; these self-sufficient techniques are called *flesh*. They aren't who we are, but only how we function when we are not trusting the indwelling Christ to meet our needs. A man who was an alcoholic before he became a Christian may still have a propensity toward physical and psychological addiction to alcohol, but that has nothing to do with his identity. Rather, it has everything to do with his *flesh*.

Lies That Bind

It would be totally inaccurate for Dirk to introduce himself by saying, "Hi, I'm Dirk and I'm an alcoholic. It's been five years and four months since I had my last drink." Does that sound like *freedom* to you? In no way do I intend to minimize the seriousness of a person's addiction to alcohol, but in God's grace-land, we have a new freedom from the shame of our past. I'm grateful for organizations that help patch people back together when they're coming apart, but Jesus Christ can do more than patch people back together. Some people who used to be addicted to *drinking* alcohol have now become addicted to *talking about* alcohol in meetings with others who have had similar struggles. Their lives still seem to revolve around alcohol, even though they don't drink it anymore. Does this sound like the best answer to you? A better option is to appropriate by faith the new identity that Christ gave you and allow Him to completely roll away the shame of the past!

My friend Mike Quarles became addicted to alcohol after he served as a pastor for a number of years. He found freedom only through understanding his identity in Christ. In his book *Freedom from Addiction,* he lists 30 different ways he tried to overcome his bondage to alcohol, including Christian counselors, psychiatrists, accountability groups, treatment centers, willpower, and many other sincere efforts.[3] It was only when Mike came to understand that his old identity had died at salvation and that he had a brand-new identity in Christ that he experienced the freedom that had been his all along. He writes of that moment when he *knew* his true identity:

> At that moment the lights came on and I understood the truth. I knew I had died with Christ. The old sin-loving sinner had died and was no more. For many years I believed I was a sinner and acted like it. Now I knew that I was dead to sin whether I acted like it, felt like it, looked like it or anyone else believed it because God said I was. I also knew the truth that I was free, "because anyone who has died has been freed from sin" (Romans 6:7 NIV).
>
> Jesus said, "Then you will know the truth, and the truth will set you free" (John 8:32 NIV). I had believed I was a hopeless, helpless alcoholic. For years I lived in bondage, but less than 24 hours away from being drunk, I knew without any doubt that I, Mike Quarles, was a child of God who was "in Christ." I had died with Christ, and was dead to sin and had been freed from sin. At last, I was free. Praise God I was free at last![4]

I have genuine compassion for those whose addiction is alcohol because I too have experienced addictions of different sorts. While alcohol hasn't been my particular area of vulnerability, I do know what it is like to struggle in other areas. I'm not pleased to acknowledge that I sometimes don't act like who I know I am. I know what it is to face temptation and lose the battle at times. Yet I know my flesh patterns are not who I am. Our fleshly behavior is inconsistent with our true identity because our old man is dead and the shame of our past is forever gone.

Dirk and Mike can never be alcoholics again. According to 1 Corinthians 6:9-11, alcoholics don't go to heaven. These men have been washed, sanctified, and justified. Could they *act* like alcoholics again if they made that choice? Of course. However, that wouldn't change their true identity. They would only be Christians *acting* like alcoholics.

> *In God's grace-land, we have a new freedom from the shame of our past.*

Sometimes it seems that the modern church is particularly hard on those who have abused alcohol. If we are going to insist that they identify themselves by their own particular sin, why don't we be fair about it and make *everybody* acknowledge their own brand of flesh when introducing themselves? Imagine this scene next Sunday at church: "Hi, I'm Sue and I'm a gossip. It's been three days since I've talked about anybody at church." "Hi, I'm Jim and I'm a lust-filled man. It was last Sunday when I last had sexual fantasies about any of the ladies here." That would really be horrible, wouldn't it? Then why single out the sin of alcohol abuse? Whether your past includes alcohol, gossip, lust, or anything else you can name, it has been rolled away by the cross! In the new land, you are free from the shame and power of your past. It is still possible to lapse into sins that characterized your life then, but it's not who you are today. You no longer live there.

What a relief it must have been for Israel to hear that the reproach of the past was gone. The sins of murmuring, unbelief, idolatry, disobedience, rebellion—all of it was gone! Now the people could move forward to possess the land with a clear conscience. Nobody can live in consistent victory without a clear conscience. But the God of the old and new covenants is just that kind of God. He will free us from the guilt of our past, give us a brand-new identity, and then lead us forward into victory. As Israel was soon to discover, the *way* to victory certainly didn't happen the way any man would have planned it.

Dear Father,

Thank You that by the cross You have forever put away my past life. I praise You that my new identity isn't determined by what I do or have done in the past. Teach me how to move forward in grace, trusting You to bring healing to my life wherever it is needed. I accept by faith that You have rolled away the shame of my past. I will accept that truth by faith even during the times that I don't feel it. Thank You, Father.

G.R.A.C.E. Group Questions

1. Read Joshua 5. Why was it important for the Jewish men to be circumcised once they had entered Canaan? Read Colossians 2:11. Explain what Paul meant when he said that Christians are circumcised by God.

2. Read Romans 6:1-6. Paraphrase the passage in your own words. What part of us died with Jesus on the cross? Does a Christian still have a sin nature?

3. Read 1 Corinthians 6:9-11. Can a Christian be an adulterer? A homosexual? A drunkard? Do any of these inherit the kingdom of God? Can a Christian behave like one of these? What would you tell a person who said his dad was a Christian but died as an alcoholic?

4. List three common lies that bind the average Christian today.

5. Find three verses not mentioned in this chapter that indicate that the old sin nature has died.

We Don't Work for God Anymore

I WAS ON A FLIGHT FROM BANGKOK, Thailand, to New Delhi, India, when I began to talk with Amit, a thirtyish man who was returning home from a business trip. He asked me what I did— the universal question the world asks to determine one's value as a person. I told him that I was a Bible teacher. "The Christian Bible?" he asked.

"Yes," I told him.

Without any hint of trying to be offensive, but rather just to make conversation, Amit said, "I don't like religion."

"I don't either," I replied.

He ignored my remark and continued, "Religion is the cause for many wars."

"You're absolutely right," I answered. "And not just between different religions, but even within the same religion."

Amit looked a little puzzled. "I think the Christian religion tries to control people," he said.

"Oh yes, you are right about that," I answered. "The Christian religion is terrible about that."

Amit turned and looked at me. "What did you say you do?"

"I teach the Bible," I answered again.

"But it sounds as if you don't like religion either," he answered.

"I don't," I said. I could see the wheels turning in his mind. "Amit, what I teach is the truth about Jesus Christ. There's a big difference between the Christian religion and biblical Christianity."

In the next hour or so, Amit and I discussed the differences between religion and a personal relationship with Jesus Christ. I explained that many people embrace the Christian religion by simply trying to live by the Bible, much like the Islamic people try to live by the Koran. I explained to him that real Christianity means sharing in a literal union with Jesus Christ, which comes by trusting Him and receiving His Life.

As we approached the airport at New Delhi, Amit said something that touched me. He said, "I never knew that there was a difference between Christianity and the Christian religion. Now I understand. The Christian religion means that a person tries to serve God by obeying the teachings of the Bible, but Christianity means that by faith a person absorbs the life of Jesus Christ into his consciousness and that Christ begins to live through him from that day forward." *Wow!* I thought. *He understands the meaning of authentic Christianity better than I did for 29 years after I became a Christian!*

Amit is not unusual in his understanding of Christianity. Most people think that the essence of Christian living means finding out what the Bible says we should do and then striving to do it. Many unbelievers hope to get into heaven because they "try to live by the Bible." Their efforts, however, are futile. Nobody can earn heaven by trying to do the things that God requires. The only entrance into heaven is found by faith in Jesus Christ.

It is also strange that the same Christian who knows that he didn't *become* a believer by working for God often believes that *after* he becomes a Christian, his whole life should revolve around working for God. He knows that he was saved by grace through faith, but believes that now the ground rules are different. This kind of Christian often studies the Bible to get instructions concerning what God expects of him now that he is saved. He understands the fact that the efforts of an unsaved man will produce no spiritual progress, but believes that his own efforts *will* yield spiritual results. He is sincere in trying to advance spiritually, but he is sincerely wrong. Self-effort will never yield spiritual fruit, but only a deep sense of frustration. We don't earn victory in the new land. It comes to us as a gift and can be received only by faith, not by our own self-effort, regardless of how heartfelt and sincere we may be.

There's a big difference between the Christian religion and biblical Christianity.

Watchman Nee wrote:

> We know that justification is ours through the Lord Jesus and requires no work on our part, but, we think sanctification is dependent on our own efforts. We know that we can receive forgiveness only by entire reliance upon the Lord; yet we believe we can obtain deliverance by doing something ourselves. We fear that if we do nothing, nothing will happen. After salvation the old habit of "doing" reasserts itself and we begin our old self-efforts again. Then God's word comes afresh to us: "It is finished" (John 19:30). He has done everything on the Cross for our forgiveness and He will do everything in us for our deliverance. In both cases, He is the doer. "It is God that worketh in you."[1]

Welcome to God's Grace-Land

The children of Israel had barely entered the land of Canaan when they realized that there was going to be resistance to their advance. The land was inhabited by pagan people who had no plans to hand over the deed to the property without a fight. As the Jews moved inland from the banks of the Jordan River, the first city they came to was Jericho. The residents of Jericho knew that the people of Israel had arrived; consequently, the city "was tightly shut because of the sons of Israel; no one went out and no one came in" (Joshua 6:1).

This was a pivotal moment in the life of Israel. How she approached the fortified city of Jericho would set a precedent for the future battles she faced. God had brought the people into the land, and now they had to decide whose responsibility it was to lead them *through* the land. Lest there be any doubt about God's plan, He spoke concerning Jericho:

> *See, I have given Jericho into your hand, with its king and the valiant warriors. And you shall march around the city, all the men of war circling the city once. You shall do so for six days. Also seven priests shall carry seven trumpets of rams' horns before the ark; then on the seventh day you shall march around the city seven times, and the priests shall blow the trumpets. And it shall be that when they make a long blast with the ram's horn, and when you hear the sound of the trumpet, all the people shall shout with a great shout; and the wall of the city will fall down flat, and the people will go up every man straight ahead* (Joshua 6:2-5).

God made it clear that Israel's victory at Jericho and at every point along their journey would be the result of *His* work, not theirs. He said, "I have *given* Jericho into your hands." All of Canaan was a *gift* to Israel. The only way the Israelites entered in was because they finally believed God and realized the only way they would move forward would be by faith. Not only would their own self-effort fail to help gain victory in Canaan, it would actually impede the victory. They didn't have to do anything for God in Canaan; He had already done it all for them. This was God's land of grace, and in this land, He does it all. His people are simply grateful beneficiaries of His goodness. Israel had moved into the land by grace and would now move *through* the land by that same grace.

Rest Is a Gift from God

It took Israel 40 years to enter Canaan because they refused to believe that God had simply *given* them the land and that all they needed to do was receive it by faith. For 40 years, "we see that they were not able to enter because of unbelief" (Hebrews 3:19). While they struggled in the wilderness, God's desire was that they enter His rest. The book of Hebrews refers to Canaan as a type of the rest believers have in Christ (see Hebrews 3:11,18; 4:1,3,8-11).

It is amazing how the default setting in contemporary Christian culture tends to oppose the concept of rest, when that is exactly what Jesus promised to give to those who follow Him (see Matthew 11:28-30). Just as God called Israel to a land of rest, we are being called to a place of rest today. This concept requires a new mind-set for most people, especially in Western culture. We live in a society where people go on vacation with their cell phones, Palm Pilots, and laptop computers. To rest in Christ—to trust Him to express His life through us—sounds lazy and negligent after we have lived in the wilderness of rigorous religion for such a long time. Many mistakenly think of rest as some sort of passivity, which it is not. Rest means to trust Jesus Christ as our Life-Source, depending upon Him to empower our actions with His strength and direction.

As a legalist, the concept of rest was so foreign to me that I couldn't comprehend it. I didn't know rest was a gift from God. I thought it was a sin. I sincerely believed that the only time we would find complete rest was when we died and went to heaven. There was a verse I used to read at funeral services to give comfort to bereaved families. I would share Hebrews 4:10 with them: "For the one who has entered His rest has himself also rested from his works, as God did from His."

When I shared this verse, I would tenderly point out that our beloved friend who had died "has now entered into God's rest and ceased from his own labors." I talked about how heaven is a place where there are no more struggles. It is a place where we simply rest in Christ and enjoy Him forever.

For years, the idea of entering into God's rest and ceasing from our own works sounded like dying and going to heaven to me. Then one day I read the *next* verse in the passage—Hebrews 4:11, which says, "Let us therefore be diligent to enter that rest, lest anyone fall down through following the same example of disobedience." What? Be diligent to enter *that* rest? Now I was in trouble. I had always taught that rest meant dying. Now here I was being confronted with the verse that says to be diligent to enter that rest or else I would be disobedient to God. I knew I had to go back and reexamine that verse again and hope that my interpretation had been wrong or else I was in serious trouble! I didn't know at the time that I had *already* died with Christ and was able to cease from my own works.

Our Part and God's Part

"I understand that salvation is a gift, but when we become Christian we have certain responsibilities in living the Christian life, don't we?" Kelly asked. "We don't just sit back and coast to heaven with no obligations in the meantime." Kelly's concern is common. Her statements reflect a belief that if we don't take ownership of certain things that we must do for God, we may become passive and lazy.

What is the responsibility of the believer toward God? The disciples once asked Jesus about the works they were to do for God. "They said therefore to Him, 'What shall we do, that we may work the works of God?' Jesus answered and said to them, 'This is the work of God, that you *believe* in Him whom He has sent' " (John 6:28-29, emphasis added). When asked what we are supposed to do in order to do the work of God, Jesus gave one work: *believe.* If we are to take the words of Jesus at face value, then faith is the sole work of the Christian (and even that is a gift from Him—see Ephesians 2:8). That fact doesn't mean that nothing else will be done, but that nothing else *can* be done unless it flows from the abiding relationship of faith in Him as our constant Life-Source (see John 15:5). As we trust Him, we will discover the reality of the truth "faithful is he that calleth you, *who also will do it*" (1 Thessalonians 5:24 KJV, emphasis added).

The reason that Israel would possess Canaan wasn't because of any work they had done, but because of the promise God had made to Abraham many years earlier (see Genesis 12:1-3). It wasn't because of *their* work, but *God's,* that they would be blessed. It was only by God's doing that they would enjoy abundance in life. It would happen because of the covenant He had made with them through their father, Abraham.

Christians Are a Covenant People

God has made a covenant with believers today. Just as was the case with the one He made with Abraham, the responsibility for fulfilling the covenant depends on His works, not the works of man. We are simply to receive His grace gifts by faith. The same rest that He offered to Israel is promised to us. Don't think that God's offer of rest ceased when Israel entered Canaan: God has a bigger plan in mind than simply the one He has for the nation of Israel. That plan includes you.

The writer of Hebrews said, "If Joshua had given them rest, He would not have spoken of another day after that. There remains therefore a Sabbath rest for the people of God" (Hebrews 4:8-9). There is a rest that's bigger and better than Canaan; it is the rest that we can experience through our life in Christ. Canaan is like a glimpse at a 50¢ postcard from Hawaii while being "in Christ" is living in a luxurious beach house on Maui—there's just no comparison! Experiencing His life surpasses anything that Israel could have known in the promised land. There's nothing we can do to earn it; we can only accept it as a gift.

One passage that so clearly illustrates the unilateral nature of God's grace is found in Genesis 15. After taking Abraham outside at night and telling him to count the stars in the sky, God told him, "So shall your descendants be" (15:5). Abraham believed God but couldn't imagine how such a thing could happen since he had no children at all, and he was an old man. God then gave him instructions that seem strange to our modern-day minds:

> "Bring me a three year old heifer, and a three year old female goat, and a three year old ram, and a turtledove, and a young pigeon." Then he brought all these to Him and cut them in two, and laid each half opposite the other; but he did not cut the birds (Genesis 15:9-10).

This may sound like a strange and gruesome scene, but it made perfect sense to Abraham. He understood that God was about to ratify a covenant.

This was a common manner in which covenants were made in Abraham's day. Sacrificial animals were divided into halves with an open pathway left between them, and the two parties who entered into a covenant passed between them together to seal their agreement. The ratifying of a covenant was much stronger than making a contract. The blood present at the ratification of the covenant indicated that the parties who passed between would be willing to fulfill their terms of the covenant even if it cost them their own lives.

Rest means to trust Jesus Christ as our Life-Source, depending on Him to empower our actions with His strength and direction.

In the Bible, *nothing* was more serious than a covenant. In a contract men agree that both parties will do their part. If one fails to live up to his part of the deal, the contract becomes null and void. However, when one entered into covenant with another, he was indicating that he would fulfill his part *regardless of what the other person did.* Contracts are a 50-50 proposition, but when a man makes a *covenant,* he is affirming that he will give 100 percent toward his commitment even if the other person gives absolutely nothing.

As Abraham prepared the sacrifices for the covenant, he must have felt great anticipation about entering into a covenant with God. However, as the time drew near for the covenant to be ratified, an unexpected turn of events occurred. "Now when the sun was going down, a deep sleep fell upon Abram; and behold, terror and great darkness fell upon him" (Genesis 15:12). When God was ready to seal the covenant, He caused Abraham to fall into a deep sleep.

"And it came about when the sun had set, that it was very dark, and behold, there appeared a smoking oven and a flaming torch which passed between these pieces. On that day the LORD made a covenant with Abram..." (Genesis 15:17). The smoke and fire that appeared were the manifest presence of God. It is notable that in this instance, only one symbolic representative of the parties passed between the halves of the animals. The only one to pass through the halves was God. The covenant was to be kept from the Godward side alone. Only the Lord Himself could fulfill its promises.[2]

God Does It All

Don't miss the significance of God's covenant with Abraham. Israel missed the point and it cost them 40 years in the wilderness. When the time came for the covenant to be ratified, God caused Abraham to fall asleep for an important reason. There was no way that Abraham could live up to the promises he would have been making by passing through the sacrifices. It was as if God were saying, "Abraham, I know you have good intentions, but there is nothing you could ever do for Me. You would only break any promises you make. So for that reason, I want you to lie down and *rest* while I ratify the covenant. I'll do all the work. You simply trust Me and be the recipient of all I do."

Abraham had believed that he and God were going to enter into a covenant together, but God knew that a bilateral covenant would only set Abraham up for failure. So instead of them making a covenant *together,* God committed to the covenant for both of them, assuming responsibility for fulfilling both sides of

WE DON'T WORK FOR GOD ANYMORE

the covenant. Abraham's sleep was a foreshadowing of the rest that we experience in Christ. Any covenant we have with God *must* be one-sided because we totally lack the ability to live up to any commitments we make.

Many Christians have misunderstood the new covenant. They think salvation works like this: God forgives us for all our past sins. He now asks us to serve Him through our actions. He gives us a Bible to tell us *how* to live for Him. He offers to help us do the things we need to do anytime we ask Him. They believe that He forgave us; that was His part. Now we are to live for Him. That's our part. Right? Nothing could be further from the truth! If we couldn't save ourselves to start with, what makes us think we can live the Christian life now that we are saved?

For us to believe that we can live the Christian life is comparable to Abraham thinking that he had what it took to father a whole nation. He was 100 years old when Isaac was born. One hundred years old! It doesn't take a genius to figure out that at that age a double dose of Viagra, a trip to Fredericks of Canaan, satin sheets, soft music, candlelight, and a willing wife just weren't enough! He might give it the old college try, but apart from a miracle from God it just wasn't going to happen. Either God had to assume responsibility for it all, or the covenant wouldn't be fulfilled.

The Way to Victory

"What do you mean I need to rest in Christ?" Rodney asked. "I'm the head of the outreach committee in our church. If I rest, who will lead the effort to reach the unchurched in our community?" Rod's question resonated with me, reminding me of my own past experience in ministry. For many years I had reasoned that there was no time for rest. After all, I was in ministry and there were places to go, things to do, and people to see. My life was illustrated in a poem I once heard that says, "Mary had a little lamb; it used to be a sheep. Then it joined the local church and died from lack of sleep!" I used to say that I'd rather burn out for God than rust out. Then one day the Lord caused me to realize this: "Either way, you're *out*." I now know that God doesn't want us to burn out, but to burn *on*. Rodney's concern that the work of God would go undone if he rested is shared by many believers, but it simply isn't true. To rest in Him is to be both empowered and motivated by Him.

Those who trust in the Lord as their Source are active, but their activity is propelled by a power outside their own—thus they rest and work at the same time.

A recent article in a leading Christian periodical wrestled with the matter of how we are to rest in Christ and still be consistent in our spiritual service. The author concluded that what we need is balance, reserving a time for resting at the feet of Jesus and a time for working out in the field. This author's viewpoint is common in the contemporary church, but it misses the essential element of resting in Him. It isn't necessary at any given moment to choose between resting in Christ and serving Him. It is possible to do *both* simultaneously. Isaiah 40:31 says, "Those who wait for the LORD will gain new strength; they will mount up with wings like eagles, they will run and not get tired, they will walk and not become weary." Those who trust in the Lord as their Source are active, but their activity is propelled by a power outside their own—thus they rest and work at the same time.

The way to victory is to rest in Christ by recognizing Him to be our very Life. It is to realize that in God's grace-land, we do not work for Him, but rather we allow Him to do the work Himself *through us*. Jesus wants us to recognize our complete insufficiency to produce works that have eternal value. He wants to be the One who does the works through us as we renounce our own self-sufficiency and depend continuously on Him.

It is obvious that God didn't cause Abraham to become the father of a great nation without His involvement. The source of Abraham's capability to father children in his old age was the divine enablement of God, not Abraham's sufficiency for the task. When Isaac was born, Abraham never fancied himself to be a "lean, mean love machine." He knew the Source of his sufficiency. It was pretty obvious to everybody how it had all happened. It was God's doing. The way to victory for Abraham was by faith and faith alone.

Choosing What We Are Going to Believe

As the people of Israel faced the fortified walls of Jericho, they had to decide what they were going to believe. They could have reasoned that God had been good enough to lead them across the Jordan River and into the promised land, and it was now up to them to conquer the city by their own determination and commitment.

Fortunately, Israel did not take that approach, as logical as it might have seemed. Instead, they chose to believe God's statement that He had indeed given them Jericho as a gift. They didn't ask Him to help *them* flatten the city walls, but simply followed God's instructions on how to proceed. They *rested* in Him, moved forward in complete obedience, and trusted Him to do the work. Consequently, God *did* do the work and they simply reaped the benefits.

What a life we have been given in Christ! He does the work and we get the benefits. How different this new land is from the wilderness of religion, where blessings are directly commensurate with our own self-effort. When we lived in the wilderness, blessings were a reward for faithfulness. Here in God's grace-land they are an unconditional gift. In the wilderness, our works were of primary importance. In grace-land it is *His* work that becomes the focal point of life. The only thing we need to do is learn how to live in this new world, a lesson that sometimes isn't learned easily, as Israel was about to find out.

Dear Father,

For too long my focus has been on what I should do for You. I realize now that the good news of the gospel is in what You have done for me! Thank You for everything You have given to me in Christ. Teach me how to actively trust in You, depending upon You to do the things in me and through me that You want to accomplish.

G.R.A.C.E. Group Questions

1. Discuss five differences between Christianity and the Christian religion. How does a Christian become vulnerable to becoming involved in the Christian religion and losing his focus on Christ?

2. Read Joshua 6:2-5. List three similarities between how God gave the victory to Israel at Jericho and how He wants to give victory to Christians today.

3. What does it mean to rest in Christ? What is the difference between resting in Him and being passive? What keeps the believer from the danger of passivity?

4. What is man's part in salvation? What is the Christian's part in the process of his own spiritual growth?

5. Read Genesis 15. What part did Abraham play in the covenant God made with him? What part do Christians have today in the new covenant?

$\mathcal{O}$ur Personal Best Will Ruin Us

"I CAN'T BELIEVE I MADE SUCH A foolish choice! I *know* who I am in Christ. I understand what it means to have Him live through me. How could I fail so miserably?" Brit had come to understand his identity in Christ only a few months earlier. At that time, I had been seeing him and his wife to counsel them about problems they were having in their marriage. During the time we spent together, Brit had come to see that a big part of the problem was the way he tried to control his wife. He had a history of being sarcastic and critical when he didn't like something she did.

Jana was a quiet lady who struggled with feelings of inferiority. Whenever Brit went into his attack mode, she would generally give in to whatever he wanted her to do, then withdraw—refusing to communicate for days. Over the seven years they had been married, this pattern had repeated itself many times until they both had come to the place where they thought the best solution might be for them to go their separate ways.

They had come to see me for counsel on the recommendation of a friend. Never had I seen two people who were more ready to receive the truth about their identity in Christ. Both of them had been convicted of the way they consistently acted toward each other and had quickly come to the place where they understood what it means to abide in Christ, allowing Him to control their lives and marriage.

Now, less than three months later, Brit sat before me in obvious despondency. "Last night, I did it. Jana didn't agree with me on something I felt strongly about, and I blasted her. I didn't stop until she left the room crying. I apologized this morning, but she won't talk about it. That's when I called you. Right now I hate myself."

Trouble in Paradise

Before I continue with Brit and Jana, let's go back to what we've been learning about the nation of Israel in the promised land. With the taste of victory still fresh in their memories, the people of Israel moved onward from Jericho to the next city in their path. As they drew near to Ai, Joshua sent ahead a small unit of men who would spy out the land in order to determine what resources were needed to ransack Ai. Shortly afterward, the men returned with their recommendation: "Do not let all the people go up; only about two or three thousand men need go up to Ai; do not make all the people toil up there, for they are few" (Joshua 7:3).

At their advice, Joshua sent 3,000 men up to Ai to overthrow the city. In no time, the army of Israel came running back down the hill to their camp. Their report was tragic: The campaign had been a total loss. Not only had they failed to defeat the city, but 36 of their own men had been killed in battle. Breathless, the men explained how they themselves had barely escaped with their own lives.

It was at this point that Joshua fell on his face in prayer, asking the question posed by most believers when we suffer defeat: "O Lord God, why...?" (Joshua 7:7). In Joshua's case, the answer was apparent. God had specifically told the people not to touch any of the spoils of battle when they conquered Jericho. His purpose was that the whole city should be set apart to show that it was not by Israel's power, but by His own, that Jericho would be overthrown (see Joshua 6:17-19).

In defiance of God's command, one of the Israelite soldiers violated the ban and took some of the things that God had clearly marked as His own. He acted independently and took some of the spoils, despite what God had said. His independence cost Israel dearly. Men died, and a nation of people were confounded. Perhaps when Achan stole the goods he thought that his action was insignificant. He might even have justified his behavior by reasoning that with so much wealth in Jericho, his decision to take a garment and a little silver and gold would make no difference whatsoever.

> *The same dependent faith on God that was required to bring us safely into the land is necessary to guide us victoriously through it.*

Though God had miraculously led Israel into the paradise that had been promised to them since the time of their father Abraham, that didn't exempt the people from the possibility of failure. Likewise, both Brit and Jana, when they came to me again for marital counseling, were beginning to realize that just because God has led us into His land of grace, that doesn't exempt us from the possibility of failure. The same dependent faith in Him that was required to bring us safely into the land is necessary to guide us victoriously through it.

When I began to understand my identity in Christ, I first thought that I would never come down off the mountaintop experience I was enjoying. I was so thrilled about my newly realized understanding of my identity in Christ that I thought I would never falter in battle again. After all, Jesus would fight my battles, thereby ensuring my ongoing victory. However, just as Brit and Jana learned, I soon began to discover that walking in grace doesn't mean that we don't still face the potential for defeat. Like Achan, I underestimated the potential harm from acting independently of God.

One might wonder how Achan could rebel against God after having seen Him work on behalf of Israel in such a miraculous way at Jericho. It would be wise, however, not to be too harsh in our judgment of Achan. While his behavior can't be excused, the truth is that we have all known the experience of having failed. Each of us can relate to the kind of shame Brit felt after he had mistreated his wife.

What causes people who have seen God work in their lives in such a powerful way to choose at times to act independently of Him? If the old man we were in Adam is indeed dead, then why do we still sin?

We Must Understand the Battleground

Perhaps it would be helpful for us to clearly understand the meanings of some common terms in order to clarify why we as believers still sin at times despite the fact that our very nature is holy. We do have the potential to say no to temptation every time we face it, but a lack of understanding of where the battle lies for the believer has led many to defeat. If we don't understand the method of operation used by the enemy in his attacks, we will always be vulnerable. Any enemy has the advantage when attacking under the cover of darkness. To be equipped to sustain victory in our own battles in the new land, it's important for us to understand the meaning of certain words so that we know the terrain of the place in which we now live. Consider these three terms and their meaning:

The sin nature—this is the nature possessed by every person who is in Adam. It is the nature of the unbeliever (see Ephesians 2:2-3). At salvation, God puts one's sin nature to death so that it no longer exists within him (see Romans 6:1-3; 6:6; Galatians 2:20; Colossians 3:3). This was discussed in depth in chapter 4. Much confusion has been caused in the minds of many believers because of the choice by the New International Version translators to render the Greek word *sarx* (flesh) as "sinful nature." These brethren were undoubtedly sincere in their effort toward accuracy in translation, but they simply dropped the ball on this one. If you read the NIV, don't be confused when you come to the phrase "sinful nature" in your Bible. Simply substitute the word "flesh" in your mind. That's the word used in other translations and it's a better choice. Christians don't have a sin nature because it died at the time of receiving Christ.

Flesh—this is the word often used in the Bible to describe self-sufficiency. Sometimes when the word is used it may mean "skin," but often the word refers to the techniques we use to manage life (see John 1:13; Romans 7:5; 8:4-13; 13:14; 1 Corinthians 1:26; Galatians 3:3; 5:17,24; Philippians 3:34).[1] *Flesh* denotes those learned strategies we have developed for handling our lives when we aren't depending on Christ. It is learned behavior that is expressed when we live in independence. When we became Christians, our flesh didn't die. Our learned patterns of self-sufficiency remain filed away in our brains, ready to be activated at any time that we don't depend on Jesus Christ to live through us.

Indwelling sin—all Christians possess a new nature that causes them to have the desire to behave in a way that brings honor to Jesus Christ. There is, however, an indwelling force with which we must reckon. This power of indwelling sin is a force in our imperfect bodies that is always ready to pull us downward into sins. Paul personifies indwelling sin, separating its presence within him from his own true identity. Concerning the sins expressed through his behavior, he said, "So now, no longer am I the one doing it, but sin which indwells me" (Romans 7:17). Again, three verses later, he says, "But if I am doing the very thing I do not wish, I am no longer the one doing it, but sin which dwells in me" (7:20). Twice in three verses Paul points out the reality of indwelling sin.

While a Christian's old sin nature has died and Christ has become his very life, he still lives inside the same body he has always had—a body that has not yet been completely perfected. One day we will receive glorified bodies that are free from the influence of sin, but in the meantime we are confined to bodies that still bear the consequences of the sin that they still have within them.

How the Battle Is Lost

"I don't know what to do about a problem I'm having. I know the Bible teaches that my old man was crucified, but he keeps coming back to life!" I understood why Bruce would make such a statement. He didn't understand the difference between the power of indwelling sin and his old sin nature. He believed that his old man was still troubling him.

The old sin nature will never pose a problem for the believer because it has been put to death by the cross. Failure in battle comes when the Christian allows the power of indwelling sin to cause him to act out of his flesh. To function from our flesh is simply to act out of our own natural abilities instead of trusting Christ to give life to our actions.

Depending on our own natural resources usually doesn't *look* so bad if they are religious. I used to think that walking after the flesh referred to the man who stayed out drunk all night on Saturday and then showed up at church on Sunday morning with bloodshot eyes. *That* was "flesh" as I understood it. If a man was having an affair, *that* was flesh. If somebody was embezzling money from his company, *that* was flesh. It's true; all those things are an indication that somebody is living out of their self-life and not by the life of Christ. However, flesh doesn't have to look like that.

Many sincere Christians are walking after the flesh for one simple reason: they are depending on themselves to try to live the Christian life instead of trusting Christ to be the Source of their behavior. It's the same mistake Joshua made at Ai by sending spies to see what *resources* were needed to defeat the city there. We only need *one* resource in God's new land.

Charles Trumbull, while he was in Edinburgh, learned of a meeting in which the speaker was going to speak on the subject of the resources of the Christian life. He writes,

> I went eagerly to hear him. I expected him to give us a series of definite things that we could do to strengthen our Christian life; and I knew I needed them. But his opening words showed me my mistake, while they made my heart leap with a new joy. What he said was something like this: *"The only resources of the Christian life, my friends, are just—Jesus Christ."* That was all, but that was enough.[2]

Western-world Christians find that fact hard to believe. Our culture has programmed us throughout our whole lives to do our personal best, to excel by sheer effort and determination. Many have adopted that philosophy in their Christian walk, thinking that God is pleased by it. I have even heard it said that we are supposed to do the best we can, then God will take up the slack and do the rest. That is found *nowhere* in the Bible! Christians are not to live up to the best of their ability and then trust God to do *the rest.* We are to trust Him to do it *all!* Our personal best will ruin us because we aren't called to do our best, but to rely at every moment upon Jesus Christ as our Source of life. *He* is to be our personal Best. The whole purpose of Christ indwelling the believer is that we are now able to live out of *His* ability. Does this mean that our ability lies unutilized within us? Not at all. Our ability is to be energized by His life, thereby making it His ability.

> *Our personal best will ruin us because we aren't called to do our best, but to rely at every moment upon Jesus Christ as our Source of life. He is to be our personal best.*

Someone once challenged me on my assertion that we are to depend upon Christ to do all that needs to be done and not our-selves. "Even Paul said that he labored and strived in the ministry," he said.

"You are right," I responded, "but look at the *way* that Paul put forth that effort. Colossians 1:29 says, 'For this purpose also I labor, striving *according to His power,* which mightily works within me'" (emphasis added).

In no way am I advocating passivity in the Christian life. Joshua's army did indeed defeat Ai, as recorded in Joshua chapter 8. They fought in battle by setting an ambush, attacking their opponents, and overthrowing the city. However, they were quick to remember the promise of God that "the LORD your God will deliver it into your hand" (Joshua 8:7). We *do* strive, labor, fight. We *do* actively participate in what the Holy Spirit is doing in the world around us, but we do it as we depend upon His power, which works mightily in us. Concerning his own ministry, Paul said, "In Christ Jesus I have found reason for boasting in things pertaining to God. For I will not presume to speak of anything except what Christ has accomplished *through me,* resulting in the obedience of the Gentiles by word and deed" (Romans 15:17-18, emphasis added). Paul recognized that his ministry had actually been the result of Christ working through him. To live otherwise is to walk after the flesh.

The essence of flesh is self-effort, which stems from independent living. The Bible cautions repeatedly against walking after the flesh (see Romans 8:4-5,7-8; 13:14). However, many Christians spend their lives trying to find new ways to strengthen their religious flesh so that they can live the life they think God expects of them. Remember that the flesh can look *good* (see Philippians 3:4-6), but it is still flesh.

You Aren't Your Own Enemy

It is important to understand that indwelling sin in the believer's body may be *in* us, but it is not a part of our identity. It's not who we *are.* Twice Paul said that sin dwelled *in* him (see Romans 7:17,20), but he never thought for a moment that indwelling sin was a part of his identity. He didn't believe that he was an evil man simply because he at times found himself not practicing the things he wanted to do, but doing the very things he hated (see Romans 7:15). He understood that the source of his misbehavior was indwelling sin.

This fact doesn't minimize the seriousness of sin in our lives at all. In no way may we shirk responsibility for our sin because of indwelling sin. We are responsible for our own choices. However, understanding indwelling sin does equip us to experience victory over it when we come to realize that we aren't evil just because we do wrong things at times. The *deed* may be evil, but we as Christians can never be anything other than the righteous people God has created us to be.

Before I understood my identity in Christ, I often experienced self-condemnation in my life because of the sins I committed. I was an easy mark for the enemy because it took so little to cause me to feel like I must be basically evil. Perhaps I would become impatient with my children, start an argument with my wife, have a lustful thought, or commit some other sin that would cause me to go into the "God, what is wrong with me?" mode. I felt like I had a split personality, desiring at times to live a holy life and at other times wanting to act any way but holy.

I knew I was a Christian, but felt that at the core of my being there was something evil. I was completely sincere in my walk with Christ, but I saw this "evil twin" lurking within me, waiting to get out if I didn't keep a tight grip on him at all times. I thought that in some way I was my own worst enemy. I sometimes heard it reinforced by Bible teaching that cited that oft-quoted "theologian" Pogo by saying, "We have met the enemy, and he is us." I believed every word of it. After all, my experiences certainly seemed to validate that I was my own worst enemy.

Maybe you can identify with how I felt, and perhaps you still believe that way—but I hope your beliefs will be changed. Otherwise, you'll remain in the same bondage of self-condemnation that I often experienced. The truth that will set you free is this: *You are not your own enemy.* There is nothing wrong with you as a Christian. There is only something wrong *in* you, which is indwelling sin. Have you felt evil at times? That doesn't mean you are evil, but only points to the presence of indwelling sin, which is *in* you.

Paul boldly affirmed, "I find then the principle that evil is *present in me*, the one who wishes to do good" (Romans 7:21, emphasis added). He did not say that he was evil, but only that evil was present in him. Twice in one verse he cites the location of this indwelling sin, saying, "But I see a different law *in the members of my body*, waging war against the law of my mind, and making me a prisoner of the law of sin *which is in my members*" (7:23, emphasis added). Paul said the power of indwelling sin was in his body.

A couple I know recently discovered that cancer was in the wife's body. Her husband has continually kept all their friends updated on her progress through e-mail. He often described the cancer as "that invader." The cancer *is* an invader that threatened her health and had to be attacked with a vengeance by medical professionals. As her doctors ministered life to her the cancer began to disappear, and at this point, it can no longer be detected.

So it is with the power of indwelling sin, which is in our body. It is a "disease" that every one of us inherited from our father, Adam. It is an invader that will only disappear as we continually receive the ministry of the indwelling life of Jesus Christ.

Saved by His Life

Paul made an interesting observation in Romans 5:10: "If while we were enemies, we were reconciled to God through the death of His Son, much more, having been reconciled, we shall be saved by His life." In this verse he speaks of two aspects of salvation: On the one hand, he affirms that we have been saved. He says that through the death of Jesus Christ we were reconciled. It is by the death of Jesus at the cross that we have been forever delivered from the penalty of sin. However, Paul doesn't stop there, but goes on to say that "we shall be saved by His life." Not only have we already *been* saved, but we also *shall be* saved by His life. From what? From the *power* of sin. It is by the indwelling *life* of Jesus Christ that we are continually saved from it. Jesus is the miracle cure for the cancer of indwelling sin, which is in our body. All Christians have enjoyed the remedy for the penalty of sin by the *death* of Jesus Christ, but many aren't taking advantage of the ever-present cure for the power of sin in our lives. That cure is the *life* of Jesus Christ within us.

> *J*esus is the miracle cure for the cancer
> of indwelling sin, which is in our body.

As we apply by faith the sufficiency of the life of Christ over the power of sin, we will walk in victory. He has come to cause the sin of our lives to go into remission forever. Peter declared that "whosoever believeth in Him shall receive remission of sins" (Acts 10:43 KJV—in the King James Version, note the promise of the *remission* of sins in Matthew 26:28; Mark 1:4; Luke 1:77; 3:3; 24:47; Acts 2:38; Romans 3:25). Sin has no power over the believer as he rests in the sufficiency of Christ. Andrew Murray illustrates the principle this way:

I have read of a young lion whom nothing could awe or keep down but the eye of his keeper. With the keeper you could come near him, and he would crouch, his savage nature all unchanged, and thirsting for blood, trembling at the keeper's feet. You might put your foot on his neck, as long as the keeper was with you. To approach him without the keeper would be instant death. And so it is that the believer can *have sin* and yet *not do sin*. The evil nature, [of] the flesh, is unchanged in its enmity against God, but the abiding presence of Jesus Christ keeps it down. In faith the believer entrusts himself to the keeping, to the indwelling, of the Son of God; he abides in Him, and counts on Jesus to abide in Him too. The union and fellowship is the secret of a holy life: "in Him is no sin; he that abideth in Him sinneth not."[3]

When Achan's sin was discovered, the drama in Israel's story became intense. When Achan was caught, he was brought before the people with his daughters, oxen, donkeys, sheep, his tent, and all that belonged to him.

> *And Joshua said, "Why have you troubled us? The LORD will trouble you this day." And all Israel stoned them with stones; and they burned them with fire after they had stoned them with stones. And they raised over him a great heap of stones that stands to this day, and the LORD turned from the fierceness of His anger* (Joshua 7:25-26).

For many years I couldn't imagine why Israel's response to Achan's sin was so vehement, but since moving into God's graceland I have come to make better sense of what happened. Achan's sin is a picture of the flesh being activated by indwelling sin, and there is no room for a gentle approach to that. Flesh in our lives *must* be attacked with a vengeance or it will eventually destroy us.

There is no room for mercy when it comes to an attack against cancer. Similarly, the cancer of indwelling sin must be dealt with by righteous ruthlessness, lest its influence in our lives destroy our walk of victory permanently. Only fierce faith in the indwelling Christ will put the flesh into remission and allow us to walk in complete spiritual health. We aren't our own enemy; our flesh is the enemy, and it must be put down with furious faith in the One who leads us each step of the way on our journey.

Dear Father,

You know that I have sincerely tried to live as a victorious Christian. I have done my personal best, but now I realize that has been my problem—it has been "my best" that I've trusted, instead of Your life. I repent of self-sufficiency and affirm that from this moment forward I will trust You to live through me. I choose to rest in You, depending upon You to cause the power of indwelling sin in me to stay in remission. You are my Victory, oh Lord. For that fact, I thank You, Father.

G.R.A.C.E. Group Questions

1. Define these terms: the sin nature; the flesh; indwelling sin. What is the difference between the flesh and the sin nature?

2. What resources do people commonly depend upon in their efforts to live a victorious life in the modern church? What are the essential resources needed to live victoriously as a Christian?

3. Is passivity a biblical option for the Christian? Read Colossians 1:29 and discuss the method by which a believer is to serve God.

4. How does indwelling sin influence the Christian to sin? What is the cure for the adverse effects of indwelling sin in our lives?

5. Read Joshua 7:25-26. Explain what this Old Testament passage illustrates about the power of indwelling sin in a New Testament believer's life.

seven

BECAUSE OF HIS AMAZING GRACE...

God Has Finished Giving

IT WAS ON A SUNDAY MORNING that I sat in my office before the worship service began. I was thinking about the hour that was to come, hoping that we would all sense the Lord at work among us. A few weeks earlier I had done something that I thought made good sense and that seemed to create an atmosphere of expectancy among the congregation. I had asked the people to join together in prayer that God would "pour out His blessings upon us" during our time in church. This time of prayer seemed to be effective, so I decided to do the same thing again the next week, and the next. As I sat in my office four Sundays later, I thought about how I would do the same thing again in this service. It seemed that asking God to give His blessings to the church was a good way to begin any service.

As I dwelled upon encouraging the people to ask for God's blessings, a sudden thought interrupted my imaginary scene. The thought was plain: *Stop telling the church to do that.* The words disturbed me. After all, I was encouraging the people to do something good. I was tempted to dismiss this peculiar thought, when I heard it again in my mind: *Stop telling the church to do that.* "This is strange," I thought. "Lord," I asked, "is this thought from

You?" It made no sense. Why would God speak to me in my thoughts, instructing me not to tell the people to pray for His blessings?

Making no sense out of the strange thought that had entered my mind, I began to read from the Bible, Ephesians chapter 1. Soon the thought that had come to my mind made perfect sense as I read the words of the third verse: "Blessed be the God and Father of our Lord Jesus Christ, who *has blessed us* with every spiritual blessing in the heavenly places in Christ" (emphasis added). Suddenly I saw it! We didn't need to ask the Lord to give us His blessings. He was showing me in His Word that He had *already* given us every spiritual blessing in Christ Jesus!

As I went into the worship service that morning, I shared with the congregation what the Lord had just shown me. I read Ephesians 1:3 and explained that we don't need to ask for something that God has already given us. Instead I encouraged them to unite in *thanking* and *praising* the Lord for the blessings that are already ours in Christ. That day the atmosphere in our worship service was absolutely electrifying. We were consumed with the realization that in Jesus Christ we already have everything we need for time and eternity. Some time later I smiled as I read the words of Watchman Nee, who said, "If we had more revelation, we should have fewer prayers and more praises."[1] Divine revelation had certainly ruined my sensible plan and set our church free.

God Has Given Us Everything

After the bitter defeat in battle with the people of Ai, Joshua felt absolute dismay. There is no sensation quite like the sour aftereffect of a defeat caused by having made carnal choices. Achan's foolish choice had brought misery into the life of Israel, but there was no time to sit in contemplation of the past. As always, God was ready to put the past failure behind them and move His people forward into victory. As soon as Achan was put to death, God spoke to Joshua: "Do not fear or be dismayed. Take all the people of war with you and arise, go up to Ai; see, I have given into your hand the king of Ai, his people, his city, and his land" (Joshua 8:1).

God's words to Joshua were the only impetus he needed to launch forward again. "I have given into your hand the king of Ai," God had said. Armed with the truth that the victory was already theirs, Joshua immediately "rose with all the people of war to go up to Ai" (8:3). This wasn't the first time that it had been necessary for God to remind Joshua that He had already given them the land (see Joshua 1:3; 6:2) and it wouldn't be the last (see Joshua 10:8).

Christians today tend to slip backward into the idea that there are blessings God wants to give us if only we will do the right things. We fail to realize that His blessings have been provided as a gift, and gifts aren't given on the basis of merit. God didn't decide to bless us because of how wonderful we are, but because of how wonderful He is. Don't become immobilized by thinking that you don't deserve God's blessings. Of course you don't, but this isn't about you; it's about *Him!* We don't earn the blessings of God; we simply enjoy them by faith.

Every spiritual blessing is ours. What a thought! That means we are forever free from the struggle of trying to stay on God's good side so that things go well for us. The verdict is in on whether or not we are to enjoy divine blessings. God has given His final answer: We *have* been blessed with every spiritual blessing in Christ Jesus. It's done and nothing can reverse what God does— nothing. "The one who joins himself to the Lord is one spirit with Him" (1 Corinthians 6:17). We are in Christ and He is in us, therefore all the blessings contained in Him already reside in us. They have been "given into our hand." F. J. Huegel wrote:

Canaan represents the highest union with Christ, the Throne-life to which every believer is called. Joshua represents the Holy Spirit who quickens and imparts faith and leads the believer into this union with Christ. The Canaanites, sons of Anak, Giants, etc., represent the mighty forces of evil, Satanic and otherwise, which oppose the believer in his attempt to "take" the land of promise—i.e., his place with Christ in the Heavenlies. As to Joshua the Lord said: "Every place the sole of your foot shall tread upon, *that I have given you.*" So to the believer the Spirit says: "Blessed be the God and Father of our Lord Jesus Christ who *hath blessed* us with all spiritual blessings in heavenly places in Christ." It is held in trust. It is already the believer's *judicially,* and will become his *actually* upon the exercise of faith.[2]

God's blessings are already ours. All we need to do is believe God in order to realize them.

We didn't need to ask the Lord to give us His blessings. He was showing me in His Word that He had already given us every spiritual blessing in Christ Jesus!

When the Bible says that God has already given Christians every blessing in Christ Jesus, exactly what blessings does it mean? How can we begin to understand the full impact of God's grace in our lives? It isn't possible. Peter described it as "the manifold grace of God" (1 Peter 4:10). The word "manifold" means multifaceted, like the many fine cuts on a beautiful diamond. When one examines a flawless diamond under a bright light, its beauty may appear to be awesome. Then when the diamond is turned slightly so that the light is focused on a different facet, it may appear to be a totally different diamond, whose beauty looks to be equal to or even surpass what was previously seen. So it is with the grace of God. Christians will spend eternity marveling at this amazing grace as we continually examine it under the resplendent light and glory of the Son!

We Don't Need to Keep Asking for Blessings

Imagine the Jews going across Canaan, begging God all the way: "Lord, will you give us this city? Now will you give us that city? What about the next one?" That approach would have demonstrated the kind of bankruptcy of faith that kept them out of Canaan for 40 years. They didn't have to ask God to give them city after city. The cities were already theirs because He had told them, "I have given you this land." So has God given to the Christian everything in Jesus Christ. If you possess the life of Jesus Christ, God has finished giving because there is nothing left to give. In Jesus Christ dwells the *fullness* of deity and we have been made complete in Him (see Colossians 2:9-10).

While it isn't possible to list an inventory of the infinite blessings that are ours in Christ, there are some remarkable blessings that have been given to the church, which many Christians fail to realize are already theirs. Many continually ask God to give them specific things that He has already given to every believer. While their approach may seem right, it is actually an act of *faithlessness.* God has finished giving to the Christian. Our responsibility is to believe that He has already given us everything in Christ.

Mark 11:24 says, "All things whatsoever ye pray and ask for, believe that ye have received them, and ye shall have them." The statement there is that, if you believe that you already have received your requests (that is, of course, in Christ), then "you shall have them." To believe that you *may* get something, or that you *can* get it, or even that you *will* get it, is not faith in the sense meant here. This is faith—to believe that you have already got it. Only that which relates to the past is faith in this sense. Those who say "God can" or "God may" or "God must" or "God will" do not necessarily believe at all. Faith always says, "God has done it."[3]

We Have Already Been Given Holiness

Perhaps the greatest blessing given to the Christian at salvation is the one that most don't realize they already have: holiness. Ask the average person in the average church whether or not he is holy, and his response is likely to be, "I'm trying to be holy." For the Christian to suggest that he is trying to become holy is analogous to an unsaved man saying, "I'm trying to become a Christian."

Suppose Ted meets Ben at work one day and asks him, "Are you a Christian?"

"I'm trying to be," Ben responds.

Without hesitation Ted answers, "You can never become a Christian by *trying*. The only way to become a Christian is by trusting Jesus Christ to forgive your sins and give you His life. It isn't by trying, but trusting, that one is born again."

Imagine that Ben does trust Christ and is born again. The next Sunday Ted sees him at church and asks, "Are you holy?"

"I'm trying to be," Ben responds. What is the appropriate response from Ted in that situation? Many Christians would assure Ben that they are praying for him and encourage him not to give up his efforts. Such a response, however, would be a tragic error.

When a person becomes a Christian, he is *instantly* made holy because the Holy One takes up residence in his spirit, thus transforming his very nature. His soul, which consists of the mind, will, and emotions, begins to be transformed as the outworking of Christ's life brings renewal to his personality (soul). This holiness will become increasingly evident in his thoughts and deeds as he grows in grace, but his spirit becomes completely holy at the moment he receives Christ. At the core of his or her identity, every Christian is as holy as Jesus Christ because He is our very life. You are righteous because at the moment of salvation, Jesus Christ *became* your righteousness (see 1 Corinthians 1:30).

God's New House

I heard about two college students whose football team was about to get a goat as their new school mascot. There was much discussion between the two about where the goat would stay. One student said to the other, "Why don't we let the goat stay in our dorm room?"

"What about the smell?" the other asked.

"The goat will get used to the smell," the first responded.

Goats may get used to living in filth, but God won't live in any place that is unclean. Where does God live today? We find the answer in 1 Corinthians 3:16-17:

> *Do you not know that you are a temple of God, and that the Spirit of God dwells in you? If any man destroys the temple of God, God will destroy him, for the temple of God is holy, and that is what you are.*

In the Old Testament, God lived in the Holy Place. It was such a sacred place that no one was allowed inside except the high priest, who went in only one time each year on the Day of Atonement. Before he entered the Holy Place, the priest was commanded to conform to meticulously detailed instructions about *how* he was to approach the residence of a holy God (see Leviticus 16). He was required to submit to a purification process and put on sacred garments before entering the place where God lived. If an unauthorized or unclean person entered God's residence, immediate death was the result.

The New Testament reveals that God has moved from where He used to live. He doesn't live in the old neighborhood anymore. He has built a new house, where He now lives. That house is the Christian (see 1 Peter 2:5). He has taken up permanent residence inside the believer. In 1 Corinthians 3:16-17, Paul states indisputably that the Christian is holy by boldly asserting three basic facts: 1) You are the temple of God; 2) the temple of God is holy; 3) you are holy. To deny the truth of the believer's holiness in Christ is to totally reject this passage of Scripture.

Do you believe the Bible? The Bible makes clear that it isn't necessary to pray for God to give the Christian holiness. The person you were in Adam was unholy, but we learned in chapter 4 that that man is dead. As believers we have already been given a new life, and with it came the blessing of holiness. "If by the transgression of the one [Adam], death reigned through the one, much more those who receive the abundance of grace and of *the gift of righteousness* will reign in life through the one, Jesus Christ" (Romans 5:17, emphasis added). Righteousness is a gift possessed by every believer. God has already given holiness to you. You can know you are holy right now because the Bible says so (see Romans 5:19; 2 Corinthians 5:21; Ephesians 4:24).

We Have Already Been Given Victory

"Pray for me that God will give me victory over my temper," Nick told me one day. "If I don't get better control of myself, I'm going to end up losing most of my employees. I try to keep my temper under control, but the demands of our work cause the office to be like a simmering pot all the time. Sometimes I just boil over." Nick went on to say that he had bought books that outlined several different methods for trying to control one's temper, but all of them had failed.

God didn't decide to bless us because of how wonderful we are, but because of how wonderful He is.

Victory in any area of life, however, doesn't come to the believer by finding the right method. Rather, victory has already been given to us in the person of Jesus Christ (see Romans 8:37; 1 Corinthians 15:57; 2 Corinthians 2:14). We experience victory in life as we understand that when Christ gave us His life, we gained victory as a gift that is found in Him. We experience that victory as we appropriate by faith that Christ is our life and we trust Him to animate our actions (see 1 John 5:4).

I used to think that if I just *did* enough of the things that God expected, I would experience victory in every area of my life. I did everything I knew to do in order to experience victory. I read my Bible; I prayed; I memorized Scripture; I fasted; I attended church (and even preached the sermon when I got there); I gave financially; I was zealous in evangelism; I regularly attended

Bible conferences; I read three books each week written by Christian authors. I did it *all*, yet none of it ever brought consistent victory in every area of my life. I always felt like I had farther to go before I would reach the place where I believed I needed to be.

What a liberating day when I discovered that it isn't necessary to struggle to get to the place of victory. Watchman Nee advised, "Think of the bewilderment of trying to get into a room in which you already are! Think of the absurdity of asking to be put in! If we recognize the fact that we *are* in, we make no effort to enter."[4] The good news is that because believers are in Christ, we are continually in the place of victory. The only thing Nick needed was to understand his identity in Christ—to know that the old Nick, whose life would have been marked by impatience, is dead; to know that now Christ is his life and that Jesus is a *very* patient Person; to understand how to abide in Christ, allowing Him to express His divine life and patience *through* Nick on the job each day so that he wouldn't be defeated by old flesh patterns. His source of victory over his anger is Jesus Christ. He is the Victory in every area of our lives. Alan Redpath observed:

> When a Christian begins to count upon His presence, to reckon upon His victory, and to draw upon His power, it is like stepping into a totally different world! The child of God finds that his faith which has been firmly rooted at the Cross now starts to bear fruit because he is living in touch with the throne of God. Isn't it a new stage in Christian experience when we look not only back to Calvary but also up to a living Christ on the throne? We begin to draw infinite, heavenly power every moment of every day from Him, and we discover that the Christ who died for us is indeed Christ who is our life.[5]

As Christians we aren't fighting *for* victory, but *from* victory. The empty tomb is an eternal witness to the victory that belongs to those who are in Christ, the Victor of all the ages. God has already given victory to the Christian. You received the total victory for life when you received Christ by faith.

We Already Have Been Given Power

The year was 1975 and I was a young pastor, barely in my twenties. I had determined that I could be more effective in ministry if I only had more spiritual power. A friend and I agreed that we would begin to pray together continuously until we received the power from God that was necessary to serve Him with the kind of results that we desired. So we went into my office one evening to pray. We determined that we would not eat, sleep, or leave that room until we had *experienced* a divine infusion of power that would cause us to be forever changed.

Three long days later, we came out of our sequestered search for spiritual power. We felt no different, but concluded that maybe we already had the power we needed and just didn't know it. Later I came to discover that we were right. Our need wasn't to have God give us something from outside ourselves, but to understand the reality of the indwelling power we already had. Andrew Murray wrote:

> The power is Jesus; Jesus is ours with all His fulness; it is in us His members that the power is to work and be made manifest. And if we want to know how the power is bestowed, the answer is simple: Christ gives His power in us by giving His life in us. He does not, as so many believers imagine, take the feeble life He finds in them, and impart a little strength to aid them in their feeble

efforts. No; it is in giving His own life in us that He gives us His power.[6]

As a Christian, how much of Jesus Christ do you possess at this moment? All of Him, of course. How much power does *He* possess? Infinite power! Therefore, every Christian already has infinite power residing within him. In no way do I intend to denigrate experiences in which a person may become aware of God's power at work in him. I'm not against *experiences*. However, it is necessary that we interpret our experiences in the light of biblical truth. In the years since my private pursuit for power, I have certainly had divine encounters in which I was consciously aware of God's power (Jesus) working, at times in me, and at other times through me. A biblical understanding of those experiences causes me to know that I wasn't receiving something new from God that came from outside myself. I was simply experiencing the outworking of what God deposited in me on the day I was saved. God has already given Christians spiritual power; He has already given us Jesus Christ. It isn't possible that we should possess more power than that.

Bill Bright told the story of Mr. Yates, a man who lived in Texas during the time of the Great Depression. Mr. Yates bought a farm, which he diligently worked in order to make a living for his family. When the economic downturn of the 1930s struck, he fell behind on his mortgage. After several months had elapsed without him making a payment, he was contacted by a representative from the mortgage company. Mr. Yates was told his property would go into foreclosure if he didn't catch up on his payments. Despite his plea for time, he was given a deadline. The days began to wind down and the situation looked completely hopeless.

One day there was a knock at the door of his farmhouse. When he opened the door, he saw a man who introduced himself as a representative from an oil company. "We would like permission to drill on your property to determine if there is oil here," the man said. Thinking about how he would soon lose his property anyway, Mr. Yates granted permission, and a few days later, the oil company sent their crew. When they sank their drill deep into the earth, they immediately hit a gusher. Eighty-two thousand barrels of oil per day came shooting up out of the ground. Instantly, Yates had millions of dollars at his disposal.

Consider and answer this question: *When* did Mr. Yates become a millionaire? Was it at the time that the oil company struck oil? No, it wasn't. Mr. Yates became a millionaire on the day that he bought the property. Why, then, did he live in poverty for so long? It was because he didn't know what he already possessed.

As Christians we aren't fighting for victory, but from victory. The empty tomb is an eternal witness to the victory that belongs to those who are in Christ, the Victor of all the ages.

Many Christians have long lived in spiritual poverty despite the fact that the Bible teaches that we are rich in Jesus Christ. Have you unwittingly lived beneath your spiritual means? It isn't necessary to keep asking God to give us His blessings. He already has. When we understand this truth, we will be set free from an overshadowing sense of deficit in our lives. The truth that God has already given us everything in Christ will cause the Christian to become bold. It will become the catalyst that causes us to live in reckless abandonment to Him.

"I have given you." Four times God spoke those words to Joshua. They became the words that set him free to move forward in faith with boldness. He clung to the words of God and in fact encouraged the people with those words, telling them eight times, "The LORD has given..." (see Joshua 2:9,24; 6:16; 18:3; 22:4; 23:13,15-16). As Israel moved forward into the land, it was that truth that set them free from fear and doubt. Armed with that knowledge, it was now time to learn about their relationship to the laws of God, without which they would never know how they were to live in Canaan.

Dear Father,

I want to thank You that in Christ You have already given me every spiritual blessing. Renew my mind with this truth so that I will be set free from believing that I lack anything in my life. Thank You for being my holiness, my victory, my power, my everything. Teach me how to appropriate daily all that I possess in Christ Jesus. Thank You, Father.

G.R.A.C.E. Group Questions

1. Read and explain Ephesians 1:3. In what way has God given to us every spiritual blessing?

2. Read Mark 11:24. Name five blessings Christians often ask for that they have already received in Christ.

3. How does a person become holy? On a scale of 1-100, how holy are you (if Jesus Christ ranks a 100)? What would you say to a Christian who says that he is trying to become more holy?

4. If believers have already received victory in Jesus Christ, why don't they experience it in every situation of life?

5. Identify one area in your own life where you are not experiencing victory. What are the reasons you are not knowing victory? What is necessary for you to know victory in this area?

eight

BECAUSE OF HIS AMAZING GRACE...

We Are Free from Religious Rules

"I'VE SPENT MY WHOLE LIFE TRYING to do what God says. I didn't do all the things others did in college—drugs, premarital sex, the whole party scene. I have always attended church, read my Bible, prayed. I've done my best to live right, but in all these years I've never really felt like a good Christian. It seems that no matter how hard I try, there's this constant sense that something is missing in my life. Many of my friends who seem to have spent much of their lives doing their own thing have been blessed more by God than me. I don't understand it at all." As Paula spoke those words, I understood her sense of frustration. What she was experiencing were the classic effects of a legalistic understanding of the Christian life. It seemed to her that she should be blessed more; after all, she had tried harder than many to do the things she believed God expected.

After being reminded that God had already given Israel the land of Canaan, Joshua led the people farther in. The failure at Ai faded into the distance as the people traveled the 30-mile pilgrimage to the Valley of Shechem, one of the most beautiful places in Palestine. When they reached the valley, Joshua brought the people to a standstill. With Mount Ebal on one side and

Mount Gerizim on the other, the Valley of Shechem provides a natural amphitheater with such acoustics that a person can stand on the peak of Mount Gerizim and be heard clearly as he speaks softly to a person on the peak of Mount Ebal.

In that valley Joshua built an altar to the Lord, offered sacrifices, and then engraved the law of Moses into stone as the people watched. "Half of them stood in front of Mount Gerizim and half of them in front of Mount Ebal..." (Joshua 8:33). After carving the law into rock, Joshua "read all the words of the law, the blessing and the curse, according to all that is written in the book of the law. There was not a word of all that Moses had commanded which Joshua did not read before all the assembly of Israel..." (8:34-35).

Differences Between Law and Grace

As the people of Israel began their new life in Canaan, it was soon important to understand how their lives were to be led. They had wandered in rebellion for 40 years, and in the Valley of Shechem, Joshua brought their focus back to the law of God again. Standing before the people, he read every single word that God had spoken through Moses. He reminded them of the blessings of obeying God's law and the curses that would result if they disobeyed God's law.

Perhaps no area of biblical teaching about the Christian life is the focal point of more controversy than matters related to the law. Believers universally agree that keeping the law has nothing to do with salvation. We would all unanimously tell anybody who was trying to gain eternal life through his behavior that he was wasting his time and effort.

The differences of opinion about the law come in our different understandings of the Christian's relationship to the law *after* he is saved. Some people read the passage in Joshua 8:32-35, where Joshua calls the people of God back to the law, and see a paragon for today's church. In fact, across Christendom many are crying out for the church to return to God's standards for living. Many vehemently contend that the reason for the lukewarm condition of many local churches has been our wandering away from God's laws. To many, their position sounds right; in fact, at first glance, it sounds biblical. Those who hold this view often stir the emotions of sincere Christians who want to see a revival in the church, causing them to say, "Yes, let's lift up the biblical standard in the church!" Many are easily led to believe that what we need is a return to God's laws.

Living under the law means building one's lifestyle around a system of religious rules in an effort to produce spiritual progress or earn God's blessings.

Is this the real need of the church? I don't think so. Before I explain why, let me demystify the meaning of the word *legalism*. To put it in the contemporary language of the modern church, we are talking here about religious rules, both biblical and extrabiblical. As we examine the relationship of the believer to the law, don't simply think about the codified laws of the Old Testament or even just the commands of the New Testament. Living under the law means building one's lifestyle around a system of religious rules in an effort to produce spiritual progress or earn God's blessings.

The Pharisees of Jesus' day were the perfect example. Unlike the Sadducees, the Pharisees were theologically conservative. They believed every word of the Bible and even memorized much of it. At first glance, their behavior was above reproach. They didn't simply *observe* the laws of the Bible; they were so intent on adherence to a righteous standard that they even *added* rules to the laws of Scripture. They prided themselves on their good behavior.

Another group that threatened the early church with its insistence on the Christian embracing the law was the Judaizers. So pervasive was their influence in the church at Galatia that Paul was motivated to write a scathing letter to that church, denouncing the false teaching of legalism. Many have suggested that the book of Galatians was written to set straight a misunderstanding in the Galatian church about how a person becomes a Christian. That was not the issue, however. These people were *already* Christians and Paul knew it. Why would he think they were confused about how a person is saved? He was the one who had shared the gospel with them and seen them be born again. Paul didn't think they were confused about what it takes to be saved. That had been settled. Their misunderstanding was about how a person is to live the Christian life *after* he is saved. Paul's denouncing of legalism addressed the means of sanctification, not salvation.

The Judaizers had probably told the Galatian saints, "We know that you received Christ under the ministry of Paul. We are happy for you, but you need to understand that Paul is an evangelist, a church planter. His goal was to see you become Christians, but now you must grow spiritually and go forward in your walk of faith. We have come to teach you *how* to do that." It was at this point that Paul felt compelled to write and attack their teaching with a vengeance. In the first paragraph of his letter to the Galatians, he zeros in on the problem in their church:

I am amazed that you are so quickly deserting Him who called you by the grace of Christ, for a different gospel; which is really not another; only there are some who are disturbing you, and want to distort the gospel of Christ (Galatians 1:6-7).

Do We Focus on Relationship or Rules?

Paul said that the problem in the Galatian church was that the believers were *deserting* Him. They were turning away from Jesus Christ and focusing their attention on religious rules. They had understood perfectly the sole place of grace when they were saved, but now were being led to believe that their spiritual growth and maturity depended on themselves and what they did. Paul challenged them:

You crazy Galatians! Did someone put a hex on you? Have you taken leave of your senses? Something crazy has happened, for it's obvious that you no longer have the crucified Jesus in clear focus in your lives. His sacrifice on the Cross was certainly set before you clearly enough. Let me put this question to you: How did your new life begin? Was it by working your heads off to please God? Or was it by responding to God's Message to you? Are you going to continue this craziness? For only crazy people would think they could complete by their own efforts what was begun by God (Galatians 3:13 THE MESSAGE).

"How did our new life begin?" he asks them. Paul *knew* that they had indeed received new life. This proves his concern wasn't about their understanding of salvation, but about their walk. In his remarks to the Galatians, Paul makes it clear that when we place our focus on religious rules, we are forsaking Jesus Christ. Our focus is to be on our relationship to Him, not rules.

Every time the disciples started establishing rules—no children near Jesus; don't let the crowd touch Jesus; don't talk to Samaritan women; don't let people waste expensive perfumes—Jesus told them to knock it off, and His rebuke was usually followed by a lecture that said, "You still don't get it! We're not substituting religious rules with our rules. We are substituting religious rules with *Me!*" Jesus kept saying "Follow *Me*," not "Follow My rules." So most of us have spent our Christian lives learning what we can't do instead of celebrating what we can do in Jesus.[1]

It has already been mentioned that many Christians believe the reason so many local churches are lukewarm is because they have wandered away from God's laws. These Christians, often very sincere, contend that the need in the church is to return to God's law. Consider the words of Jesus to a lukewarm church in Asia Minor:

> *I know...that you are neither cold nor hot.... Behold, I stand at the door and knock; if anyone hears My voice and opens the door, I will come in to him, and will dine with him, and he with Me* (Revelation 3:15,20).

Jesus did not tell the lukewarm church at Laodicea that their need was to return to the laws of God. He told them that their need was to return to Him! Revelation 3:20 is not written to the unbeliever, although it has been used many times as an evangelistic verse. This verse was written to a lukewarm church that had shut Christ outside. Their great need was not to commit to religious rules, but to live out of the relationship they had with Jesus by appropriating the intimate union they already had objectively but weren't experiencing subjectively at the moment.

Remember Paula, who was frustrated because she had tried to do all the right things yet still felt that something was missing in her life? She was bewildered and discouraged about how her life seemed to lack the blessings enjoyed by many of her friends. She thought that based on her moral record, she was more deserving than they were. Paula had *done* the right things, but her words betrayed the fact that she believed God's blessings were somehow connected to a merit system based on behavior.

Jesus said in John 8:32, "You shall know the truth, and the truth shall make you free." Note that the truth sets us free. Nothing so holds many believers in spiritual bondage as do the lies of legalism. The only thing that will set us free from the penitentiary of legalism is the key of grace.

Jesus Didn't Come to Help Christians Keep God's Laws

The position of many in the modern church is that God has forgiven our sins and given us Jesus to help us do the things He wants us to do. These Christians spend their whole lives trying to make sure they know *what* God wants them to do and not do. Once they have found what they believe is the road to righteous behavior, they ask Jesus to help them travel that road. They totally miss the fact that Jesus didn't give us eternal life so that we would know what to *do;* He gave us eternal life so that we could know *Him* by sharing His life (see John 17:3).

One glaring problem with this approach is in finding the right road. As already mentioned, there are many varying opinions in the modern church about what constitutes godly living. What is acceptable to one group of Christians is completely offensive to another. If you are going to try to build your lifestyle around religious rules, whose rules are you going to follow? "I will live by what the Bible says," one may smugly answer. However, it should be acknowledged that all who seek to live by legalistic standards claim the Bible as their source of authority.

I was speaking on the dangers of legalism in a church, when someone approached me and said, "Steve, I want to give you something. This is what every new member receives at the church where I regularly attend. I think you'll find it interesting." I looked at the brochure she handed me, which was titled "Truth About Standards: Biblical Standards for Christians." The brochure listed 51 rules for Christians to live by in order to "keep our banner of victory waving high."[2] Below are the last nine of the 51 standards this group believes are important to godly living:

43. Biblical reason not to participate in worldly amusements, such as ball games, rodeos, circuses, racetracks, bowling alleys, skating rinks, theaters, video game rooms, etc.

44. Biblical reason not to go dancing, mixed bathing, etc.

45. Biblical reason for men to cut their hair short.

46. Biblical reason for women not to cut their hair but to let it grow long.

47. Biblical reason not to dye your hair.

48. Biblical reason not to wear clothing that pertaineth to the opposite sex.

49. Biblical reason to wear decent, modest clothes with modest styles; moderate prices and colors; decent dress lengths, sleeve lengths, and neck lines.

50. Biblical reason not to wear jewelry.

51. Biblical reason not to wear makeup.

Most evangelical Christians would consider this kind of list to be absurd—the idea that God is against ball games and rodeos? That He cares what color a lady's dress may be? It is important to realize that this list of religious rules isn't absurd to those who embrace it. They list numerous verses to prove the validity of each of their points.[3]

Having looked at this particular group's blueprint for living, I ask you this question: What is *yours?* "Oh," one may say, "I would never build my life around such a foolish list of rules. I simply try to do what the Bible *clearly* says." That is exactly what these brothers would say if questioned about their rules. The truth of the matter is that in the eyes of God, the legalism in our lives looks just as absurd to Him as theirs for one simple reason: Our lifestyle is not to be built on rules! Life is not about finding and keeping the *right* set of rules. Our life exists in our union with Jesus Christ. Everything is to flow out of that.

Jesus didn't come to help us keep the law; He came to deliver us from it. When we trusted Him by faith, the old man who was married to the law was put to death so that we have no relationship to it anymore. The law is alive, but the "old you" who was married to it is not. "You also were made to die to the Law through the body of Christ, that you might be joined to another, to him who was raised from the dead, that we might bear fruit for God" (Romans 7:4). Because of our co-crucifixion with Jesus Christ, believers have absolutely no relationship to the law at all—none (see Romans 3:28; 6:14; 7:6; 8:3-4; 10:4; Galatians 2:21; 3:13,21; 5:18; 1 Timothy 1:9). Our commitment is to Christ alone.

Does Grace Cause Us to Be Against the Law?

Sometimes those who embrace the grace of God and insist that the believer is freed from all connection to the law are accused of being against the law. *Antinomianism* is the word first made popular during the Reformation to describe those who are against the law. The word comes from two Greek words, *anti*, meaning "against," and *nomos*, meaning "law." Is it true that those who understand that Christians have no relationship to the law anymore are *against* it? Absolutely not.

> *N*othing so holds many believers in spiritual bondage as do the lies of legalism. The only thing that will set us free from the penitentiary of legalism is the key of grace.

After the apostle Paul made the bold declaration in Romans 7:1-5 that Christians are dead to the law, he asked the question he knew people were thinking: "Is the Law sin?" Then he answers (in the same verse), "May it never be! On the contrary, I would not have come to know sin except through the Law" (Romans 7:7). Paul affirms that those Christians who understand that believers are dead to the law are not against the law. They simply believe that it is important to properly understand the role of the law.

In chapter 7 of this book we clearly saw that in Christ, every believer has been made righteous. We have been given holiness as a gift in the person of Jesus. Paul plainly says in 1 Timothy 1:9, "[The] law is not made for a righteous man, but for those who are lawless and rebellious." The law is not made for the Christian. We have no relationship to it whatsoever, yet the law still remains. Occasionally I will hear someone say that the law has been done away with, but that statement is false. It wasn't the law that died, it was *you* who died! We died with Jesus Christ on the cross, thus ending our life with the law.

The law still serves a divine purpose in the world today, but its design is no longer directed toward those of us who are believers. The target of the law is the person outside the family of God. The divine intent of the law in the lives of unbelievers is twofold.

The Law Is Intended to Stimulate Sin

Many have believed that God gave His law to control sin in man, but the Bible teaches that the opposite is the case. What was God's reason in giving the law? "The Law came in that the transgression might increase; but where sin increased, grace abounded all the more, that as sin reigned in death, even so grace might reign through righteousness to eternal life through Jesus Christ our Lord" (Romans 5:20-21).

The law completes its job in a person's life when it causes him to see himself as utterly sinful and he turns to faith in Christ. Once that has been accomplished, he is no longer under the tutelage of religious rules.

God didn't give the law to subdue sin, but to *stimulate* it. Paul said that the law came into the world in order that transgressions might *increase*, not decrease. Law stimulates sin; it increases it in the lives of those who live under it. Do you know where sin gets its power? From the law! First Corinthians 15:56 says that "the power of sin *is* the law" (emphasis added). Paul said in Romans 7:5

that sinful passions are "aroused by the Law." Why would God give His law knowing that men wouldn't keep it, but that the law would only cause sin to "become utterly sinful" (Romans 7:13)? It is in order to bring men to Christ.

Trying to keep religious rules can never be a gateway to righteousness—neither before nor after salvation. The law is intended to bring the sin of an unsaved man's wicked heart to the surface. It doesn't generate sin, it only stimulates what is already there in order to make it known. If I put my thumb over an opened bottle of Coca-Cola and shake the bottle, what will happen? The cola will spew out of the bottle. Now, I didn't *create* the cola. I only gave it the necessary stimulation to bring it out of the bottle. That's what the law does in a person's life. Its intent is to cause one to see his sin and realize his need for Christ. Paul said:

> *Therefore the Law has become our tutor to lead us to Christ,*
> *that we may be justified by faith. But now that faith has*
> *come, we are no longer under a tutor* (Galatians 3:24-25).

The law completes its job in a person's life when it causes him to see himself as utterly sinful and he turns in faith to Christ. Once that has been accomplished, he is no longer under the tutelage of religious rules.

The Law Ministers Death and Condemnation

The other chief purpose of the law is to heap condemnation and guilt on those who live under its reign. The New Testament calls the law a ministry of death and condemnation (see 2 Corinthians 3:7,9). As one who was a longtime resident of the wilderness of religious legalism, I have walked with the law as my companion for many years. I have heard its whisper in my mind, constantly pointing out my shortcomings. I became so familiar with its voice that, for a long time, I made the mistake of thinking its voice inside me was my own.

When I was a pastor in local churches, I would often hear the voice of law speaking to me about my personal life and ministry. I would be reading my Bible, when law would say to me, "You seem to be spending a lot of time in the Bible lately."

"Yes," I would reply.

"Well, what about prayer?" the voice would say.

"Well, that's important too," I would respond. So I would determine to divide my time between Bible study and prayer.

Then the voice would whisper, "You must not care that the world around you is going to hell."

"Why?" I would ask. The voice would respond, "Because you're spending your time reading the Bible and praying, but you don't give evangelism much priority in your life."

"I guess that's right," I would concede. So then I would try to divide my time between Bible study, prayer, and evangelism.

The haunting voice would return: "Some kind of pastor you are. You seem to value those outside the church more than you do those elderly members you are to care for in your church." So then I would try to take more time to visit with the older members of my congregation. Then came the voice again: "Don't you care about the youth? They are the hope of tomorrow." So then I would try to reach out to the youth of our congregation. On and on this lifestyle I called "ministry" went, with the perpetual voice inside my head demanding, "More! More! More!"

Do you see the dilemma? When we allow our lives to be assessed by how well we measure up to a list of responsibilities we imagine we owe to God, we will always feel an overshadowing sense of condemnation. No Christian will ever live up to the picture of the person that law describes, because the law is perfect and thus paints a picture of a perfect person, which we must be if we are to meet its demands. When we impose religious rules upon ourselves, demanding that we perform up to a certain standard, we will discover that if we happen to jump the hurdle this time, law will simply raise the bar. There can never be a sense of satisfaction and joy when we try to live by religious rules because we can never do enough. When we walk with law, there will always be the stench of death inside us as we watch our joy waste away.

It Takes a Joshua to Guide Us into Grace-Land

Joshua called the children of Israel back to the law of God, a reminder that while Canaan is a type of God's grace-land in many ways, it is an imperfect type. Saints today are never called to the land of religious rules and regulations. Paul asked the Colossian church, "If you have died with Christ to the elementary principles of the world, why, as if you were living in the world, do you submit yourselves to decrees [religious rules], such as, 'Do not handle, do not taste, do not touch!' (which all refer to things destined to perish with the using)—in accordance with the commandments and teachings of men?" (Colossians 2:20-22). His question is simple: You have died to a system of religious rules, so why are you acting like you still have some connection to them?

The fact that it was Joshua who led Israel into Canaan is a striking illustration of how we entered into the land of grace. It wasn't possible for them to enter the land until the change of leadership from Moses to Joshua. Moses *could not* lead them into the promised land. Why? Consider the role of Moses in the life of Israel. Even until today he is primarily known as the Lawgiver. If I were to ask you to describe what you see in your mind when I say the name *Moses,* you might imagine Charlton Heston in *The Ten Commandments,* coming down from the mountain with the tablets in his hands.

For almost 40 years Moses had told the people what they needed to do, but they often rebelled against his leadership. At times he became angry and impatient with them. He told them where they needed to go, but he couldn't get them there. He is a graphic personification of the law. Trying to keep religious rules can never lead you into the abundant life that Jesus offers. They can point out where you are failing and tell you where you ought to be, but have no ability to lead you into that place.

The Old Testament name *Joshua* is the Hebrew equivalent of the New Testament name *Jesus*. It's the same name! Jesus is our Joshua. He is the One who leads us into the land of grace where God intends for us to live forever. So stop focusing on religious rules. You have died to that system. Jesus Christ is your life now. Understanding that we are dead to the law, the only thing needed to experience victory is to understand how God intends for believers to live. We live by a different kind of law, which is called the law of the Spirit of life in Christ Jesus.

Dear Father,

I see how subtly religious rules can turn my attention from You and onto my behavior. I know that You are the Source of godly living. I turn from confidence in rules and now rest in my relationship to You. Lord Jesus, You are my Joshua. I will gladly follow You into the land where I live by grace and not laws.

G.R.A.C.E. Group Questions

1. Read Galatians 3:1-3. In what ways do many in the modern church try to move forward in their lives by self-effort?

2. Read John 17:3 and 1 John 1:1-2. What is the meaning of eternal life?

3. This chapter lists "biblical standards" embraced by one group of people. Around what rules have you attempted to build your own life? Does the church you attend have a set of rules to follow? What are they? What does the Bible say about living by religious rules? (Cite references.)

4. Name and discuss two purposes of the law. Cite biblical references to prove your answer.

5. Describe how you have felt when you've tried to live by religious rules.

nine

BECAUSE OF HIS AMAZING GRACE...

We Can Do As We Please

"LAWLESSNESS! THAT'S WHAT YOU'RE teaching!" This is the kind of accusation no one wants to hear when he is teaching the Bible.

"I'm not teaching lawlessness," I responded to the pastor, whose voice had gotten louder as he talked about my teaching on legalism.

"So you're not against the law?" he persisted. "No, absolutely not," I responded. "The law is given by God and is a very good thing *in its place,* but it has no place in the life of a Christian."

The pastor simply couldn't accept what I was saying. After our conversation ended, he was still angry and I was left with that sinking feeling that comes from being blasted by someone.

In the last chapter, I presented several verses that state that Christians are no longer under the law. In church settings, where the focus is heavily centered on Judeo-Christian values, the message of freedom from the law is not popular. However, we must allow the Bible to be our final authority, even if it contradicts what we have always believed or been taught. We as New Testament believers haven't been called to religious rules grounded in Judeo-Christian values; we have been called to the Person of

Jesus Christ. "Come to *Me*" is the call from Jesus (see Matthew 11:28, emphasis added).

After Israel defeated both Jericho and Ai, Joshua turned his attention southward. By this time, five Canaanite kings had become very scared by the alliance Joshua had made with the Gibeonites (see Joshua 9). Therefore they united together to declare war on Gibeon, which immediately sent a call for help to its new ally, Joshua. Assured of God's promise of victory, Joshua came up from Gilgal, his base of operations, and defeated and chased the enemy. Then followed one of the greatest battles of all history, in which God deliberately intervened on behalf of His people. He delayed nightfall and lengthened the day in order that victory would be utterly complete and final. The five kings were captured and imprisoned.[1] Humanly speaking, the odds against the Israelites had been insurmountable. The key to their victory is found in the words "the LORD fought for Israel" (Joshua 10:14).

Our Source of Life Is Christ, Not Rules

Joshua and the Israelite soldiers were beginning to learn that the normal rules of engagement in battle don't fit when you add God to the equation. So it is for the believer who left behind the wilderness of religion. Law governs the realm outside of God's grace-land, but once we have entered into Christ, the old rules for moral living don't apply anymore.

Does it startle you to consider that rules of morality don't apply to believers? Christians aren't called to live a *moral* lifestyle. Moral living began in the garden of Eden when man ate from the *forbidden* tree—the tree of the knowledge of good and evil (see Genesis 2:16-17). Before that time, Adam and Eve didn't even know right (good) from wrong (evil). Note that the tree provided the *knowledge* of good and evil. It offered acquaintance with right and wrong, something Adam and Eve had never considered or even known to consider. Since they didn't know right from wrong, which did they do: live moral lives before the fall, or immoral? Neither; they lived *miraculous* lives. Their actions flowed from the union they shared with God. They had no relationship to rules of morality before the fall. Their behavior transcended morality as they experienced the living God as their only Life-Source. Their behavior wasn't simply good, it was *godly*—a much higher level of life than human goodness.[2]

Then came the fall of man, after which mankind's definitive question revolved around whether an action is good or evil. Many Christians today live by that question, desiring to always do right and not wrong. However, it is important to note that even good behavior might be a sin if the action in question doesn't originate from Christ's indwelling life within the believer. Any conduct that doesn't originate from our union with Him is not from faith, and "whatever is not from faith is sin" (Romans 14:23). One may keep all the religious rules he can find, and still be living in sin. "The righteous man shall live by faith. However, the Law is not of faith…" (Galatians 3:11-12). So to try to build our lives around religious rules is a sin!

Jesus Christ came to reverse the damage done by Adam. He came to restore us to God's original plan—that we should find our complete life in Him, not in rules outlining good and evil. Major Ian Thomas says:

> Beware lest even as a Christian, you fall into Satan's trap!
> You may have *found* and come to *know* God in the Lord
> Jesus Christ, receiving Him sincerely as your Redeemer,
> yet if you do not enter into the mystery of godliness and
> allow God to *be* in you the origin of His own image, you
> will seek to be godly by submitting yourself to external

rules and regulations and by conforming to behavior patterns imposed upon you by the particular Christian society that you have chosen and in which you hope to be found "acceptable." You will in this way perpetuate the pagan habit of practicing religion in the energy of the flesh, and in the very pursuit of righteousness commit idolatry in honoring "Christianity" more than Christ![3]

Major Thomas asserts that if a believer tries to do the right thing and observe all his religious rules, he may inadvertently practice the habits of a pagan. He may unwittingly commit idolatry by honoring the Christian religion without honoring Christ. Moral living can be godless living. Many religious cult members in contemporary society live moral lives above reproach, proof that God's call to the believer *must* be something more than an invitation to morality. He would never lead us down to the level of morality. We don't even *need* Christ to be moral. We can *do right* without Him, but we can't *be righteous*. We can live a *good* life apart from Him, but will never know a *godly* life.

The Subtle Substitute

Christ is our life (see Acts 17:28; Galatians 2:20; Philippians 1:21; Colossians 3:4). To become obsessed with anything other than *Him* is idolatry, even if that other obsession is religious rules. Perhaps the greatest danger in the American church is that we have lost our focus on Jesus Christ and have been focusing more on "Christian values," which is merely morality by another name.

There are morality gurus in American culture who are being touted as examples for us all, including Christians. One famous radio personality hosts a syndicated daily talk show during which she advises her callers about how they can resolve their moral dilemmas by applying the biblical laws of morality and decency. Seldom could anyone who embraces Judeo-Christian values disagree with her assessments and moral prescriptions. However, the *complete* preeminence that she gives to the place of moral (and often biblical) law is apparent. She speaks openly about her faith and active role in Judaism. She is a capable ambassador of the law. She may be the greatest preacher of morality in America today. There is only one thing missing in her religious advice—Life! With cold, hard facts she does an excellent job of telling people that they should move from the evil branch on the tree of the knowledge of good and evil to the good branch. However, the law always leads a person up the wrong tree! God wants us to live in the tree of life—the life of His Son.

> *The law is given by God and is a very good thing in its place, but it has no place in the life of a Christian.*

What people need isn't a change in their behavior. They need a new life-source. I don't blame the radio host for what she tells her callers. She is speaking from her own personal frame of reference, which is the Old Testament law. I *am* puzzled by the many Christians who applaud her work as if she were pointing people toward God's purpose for their lives. God's desire has never been to bring people to morality; it has always been to bring people to Himself through Jesus Christ. We shouldn't allow ourselves to assume that God has won the battle when a person's behavior is changed from bad to good. He longs to give every person something far greater than a clean life (by human standards). He wants to give them Christ's life.

Freedom Is Scary to the Religionist

The pastor who accused me of teaching lawlessness expressed his fear during our conversation: "If you don't teach people to live by godly principles, their behavior will become worldly. They will fail to be the righteous people that God has called us to be." I understood exactly where he was coming from because that had been my own perspective for many years. It sounded to him like I was suggesting that a Christian's behavior doesn't matter, which is not the case. The conduct of a Christian is *very* important. It should be an expression of the life of Jesus Christ within us.

The pastor's concern that people might fail without the help of religious rules shows his lack of understanding about the means by which we become righteous. We have already seen that righteousness doesn't come by what we do; it is who we *are* as believers. We aren't called to live by principles, but by the life of Jesus Christ, who is within us. As we do that, our behavior will transcend morality and will be miraculous.

Our need is simply to behave like who we are. To attempt to build one's life around principles is an attempt to live up to the same old law, called by another name. Whether law is called principles, rules, standards, or anything else, when our goal is to live up to any behavioral requirement for the purpose of making spiritual progress or gaining God's blessings, we have fallen prey to legalism.

Any fear that grace will lead to sin is unfounded. Grace never causes a person to become careless in conduct. "For the grace of God has appeared, bringing salvation to all men, *instructing us to deny ungodliness and worldly desires* and to live sensibly, righteously and godly in the present age" (Titus 2:11-12, emphasis added). When a person is abiding in Jesus Christ, trusting Him to animate his every action, he may do whatever he wants to do because the desires of Christ become his own.

God can propose *absolute* liberty to the one in whom He is so working that the innermost choice is only that which He wills for him. Having molded the desires of the heart, He can give His child unbounded freedom. There is no other freedom in the world but this. By the inwrought "fruit of the Spirit," God Himself has determined the desires of his heart. The outworking of those desires will be according to His own energizing power.[4]

The title of this chapter is not original with me. It was Augustine who first said, "Love God and do as you please." This kind of statement sounds radical outside of God's land of grace. The religionists of every generation will unanimously shriek in horror, "Do as you please?" Because of a deeply ingrained affinity for the law, they never hear the first part of the statement: *Love God* and do as you please. When a person loves God, doing as he pleases is to do that which pleases God.

How Are We to Live?

If we as believers are not to live by religious rules, then how should we live? The key to Israel's victory over the five kings in Joshua 10 was that "the LORD fought for Israel" (10:14). God led them to the place where He wanted them so that they would *experience* the victory He had already given them. There, *He* overcame Israel's enemies. Just as it had been at Jericho, there was no doubt that God was the One who had won the battle.

God's intended pattern for our lives is displayed throughout the Bible. He wants to be the Source of all our behavior. His desire is that we live by His life, depending totally upon Him to enable us to be all that He has called us to be and to do all that He has called us to do. God delights in our dependence upon Him.

To understand that we don't need to struggle to live a godly lifestyle—but can simply trust Jesus Christ to be Himself in and through us—takes tremendous pressure off those of us who have been struggling under the burden of religious rules. This revelation will cause us to experience the rest that is inherent to the gospel. Grace means that God does it all. What a relief to those of us who have lived in the wilderness of demanding religion! Donald McCullough said:

> Grace means that in the middle of our struggle the referee blows the whistle and announces the end of the game. We are declared winners and sent to the showers. It's over for all huffing, puffing piety to earn God's favor; it's finished for all sweat-soaked straining to secure self-worth; it's the end of all competitive scrambling to get ahead of others in the game. Grace means that God is on our side and thus we are victors regardless of how well we have played the game. We might as well head for the showers and the champagne celebration.[5]

The good news of grace is applicable to every child of God. We don't have to huff and puff, working to keep the rules. In the Bible, the word "gospel" means "good news," and the best news that any of us can hear is that we don't have to struggle to keep the law. God has released our obligation to the law by the cross (see Romans 7:6). There we died to the law and have been restored to the union not known between man and God since the fall. Now we live out of that oneness we share with Him.

Does a Dead Man Keep the Law?

Before Adam and Eve ate from the tree of the knowledge of good and evil, did they keep or break the law? It has already been established that their behavior wasn't moral, but miraculous. They didn't break the law; neither did they keep it. The law existed only within the forbidden tree, from which they had not yet eaten. They lived in union with God, a place where the law had no presence.

> *Jesus Christ came to restore us to God's original plan—that we should find our complete life in Him, not in rules outlining good and evil.*

Since Jesus Christ has reversed for the believer the spiritual sabotage unleashed by Adam, where does that leave us in relation to the law? Do Christians today keep the law? None would argue that we aren't to break the law, but do we *keep* it? Remember that the Christian has no relationship to the law whatsoever. Some believe that as we live in Christ, we *will* keep the law. Even after understanding my identity in Christ, I held that view for quite some time, but I have come to be convinced that this viewpoint carries a subtle danger with it. To suggest that we keep the law implies that we still have some relationship to it, albeit a positive relationship. However, the Bible teaches that we have no relationship to the law at all—neither negative (breaking it) or positive (keeping it). We are *dead* to the law.

I know someone who never breaks a single law of the land. He never drives above the speed limit, never litters, never disturbs the peace, never does anything wrong at all. One might be inclined to say that he keeps all the laws, but I could argue the point. The person I'm thinking of is my grandfather. I'll tell you one more thing about him: He died years ago. Possessing that knowledge, would you say that he is keeping the laws of the land? Probably not, because you now know that he has no relation to the laws of the land anymore. They simply have no relevance to where he lives today, in heaven. He has been "disconnected" from the law by virtue of his death. It would be absurd to insist that he is keeping the law just because he doesn't break it.

So it is with the life of a believer. We have been made to die to the law by our co-crucifixion with Jesus Christ. We have no relationship to it at all. If a believer doesn't commit adultery, murder, or countless other sins, does this mean that he is keeping the law? Not unless we take the absurd approach of evaluating his behavior on those terms. We don't live in the land of law anymore. Instead, we live in the land of grace—a place where the law has no relevance and no connection to us at all. The law ruled in the darkness of our legalistic wilderness wanderings, but we no longer live there. "He delivered us from the domain of darkness, and transferred us to the kingdom of His beloved Son" (Colossians 1:13).

Christians Live by a Higher Law

Does this suggest that the Christian lives a lawless lifestyle? Regarding any religious rules that might govern one's life, we live under a new covenant in which the law has become obsolete to us (see Hebrews 8:13). We are in Christ, who is our life. Rules have no place there because there is no *need* for law for the person who lives in union with a Holy God. The law exists in another dimension, one from which we have been removed. The citizens of God's grace-land live by a higher law called the law of the Spirit of life in Christ Jesus (see Romans 8:2). The only law of the Spirit *is* the life of Jesus Christ. The apostle Paul called it "the law of Christ" (see 1 Corinthians 9:21; Galatians 6:2). Christ is the only law by which we live, but His life is sufficient! As we depend upon Him to be our Life-Source, our behavior will be godly and righteous. It will be *miraculous* because by Him we will be equipped to live above our own human capabilities.

The law of Christ is a completely different type of law than that espoused from the standpoint of legalism. To compare the two is like comparing the law of the judicial system with the law of gravity—they just can't be related. The word *law* may be the same, but the concept is totally different. The law of Christ is not one that *insists* we behave in a certain way, but rather *inspires* us to live a godly lifestyle. It is no longer a matter of what we *ought* to do; now our choice to live a righteous lifestyle is because we *want* to do it. Don't try to lay a list of rules on a resident of the new land. He will tell you to keep your religious rules. He doesn't need them. As a citizen of grace-land, he can do as he pleases, but don't be concerned about his behavior. Watch him and you'll discover that *as he abides in Christ*, to do as he pleases is to live in godliness. Rules have nothing to do with it. Relationship is what motivates him.

Do I Have to Kiss My Wife?

Suppose I were to ask for some marital advice. The imaginary conversation might go like this: "I travel a lot, speaking in various places. I'm wondering about something. When I come home, do I have to kiss my wife?"

"You probably *should*," might be the response.

"Oh, okay," I reply. "Should it be a kiss on the mouth or on the cheek?"

"Probably on the mouth," one might answer.

"Understood," I say. "Can it be a short little peck on the lips or does it need to be one of those long, romantic, movie-type kisses?" I persist.

By now my counselor might pause and ask, "Steve, is there something *wrong* between you and Melanie?"

Who needs to ask advice like that? Not me! When I know Melanie is going to meet me at the airport, as she does each time I return home, I don't sit on the airplane as it arrives at the gate and pray, "Lord, lead me in what I should do now. Give me the wisdom to know what You want me to do and the strength to do it." It has never happened. When I see my beautiful wife, I kiss her. I mean I really *kiss* her. It's not the desire to be a good Christian husband or the goal to fulfill some responsibility in marriage that motivates me. It's love.

When a person is abiding in Jesus Christ, trusting Him to animate his every action, he may do whatever he wants to do because the desires of Christ become his own.

Don't try telling me the laws of marriage. I don't want to hear them. They have nothing to do with me. I love my wife. The same is true in our relationship to Christ. In Jesus Christ, the laws don't mean anything, but faith working through love means everything (see Galatians 5:6). Ray Stedman wrote:

> Love makes obedience easy; it is the delight of love to do what the loved one desires. Therefore, when the heart grows dull and obedience is difficult, the proper

response of the Christian is not to grit his teeth and decide to tough it out, but to remember who it is that asks this of him, and then for his sake to do it. When a Christian responds this way, he will find to his amazement that his own attitude has changed. A new outlook is born within him.[6]

The relationship we have with Jesus Christ is the impetus for a godly lifestyle. For the believer who is abiding in Christ, it is a delight, and not a duty, to live a lifestyle of obedience. Are there commandments in the Christian life? Of course; the New Testament gives commands for the believer, but because we love Jesus, "His commandments are not burdensome" (1 John 5:3). When a man is in love and his wife says, "Come here and kiss me *now!*" it won't be a burden for him to fulfill her command. There's no *law* in that command. To quote Stedman and to put it gently, when a person obeys God he will discover that "a new outlook is born within him." As the bride of Christ who *loves* Him, when the Lord tells us to do something, it is our *pleasure* to be obedient.

The Israelites moved forward toward Gibeon to face the five opposing kings and the Lord fought for them, suspending all the natural rules of engagement normally observed by an army. Their success at Gibeon was overwhelming. Judged on the basis of normal rules of battle, it made no sense. However, Joshua and his army had come to the point where they knew that when God is your Source, universally accepted rules become irrelevant.

Indeed, when God is our Source, the only thing that matters is Him. Consequently, it would seem that our greatest need may well be to grow in our knowledge of Him and how He operates in our lives—a lesson Israel was about to learn.

❦

Dear Father,

Thank You for the liberty You have given me as a Christian. I affirm that I am dead to the law and live completely by the life of Jesus Christ, who is within me. Cause me to grow in grace so that the desires of Jesus will be my constant desires. It is my pleasure to be obedient to You because I love You.

G.R.A.C.E. Group Questions

1. Read Genesis 2:16-17. What did this tree offer to Adam and Eve? Why was it God's purpose they should not eat from the tree of the knowledge of good and evil?

2. Read Galatians 3:11-12. Why is it a sin for the Christian to build his life around religious rules? Is the law sinful? Explain the purpose of the law.

3. Why is trying to get people to live by Judeo-Christian values a wrong goal for Christians? What should be the goal of believers in their relationships with those outside of Christ?

4. What is Christian liberty? Does grace imply that a believer can live a sinful lifestyle without it making any difference in his life? Read Romans 6:1-3 and discuss its meaning.

5. Do Christians keep the law? Do we break the law? Read Romans 8:2 and discuss what it means to live by the Spirit of life in Christ Jesus.

ten

BECAUSE OF HIS AMAZING GRACE...

God Never Becomes Angry with Christians

I STOOD THERE STARING AT MY CAR sitting on the side of the road. "Lord, please. Let the engine start this time." I got back into the car and once again turned the key in the ignition. The starter spun as fast as it could go, but the engine just wouldn't respond. As I sat in the car waiting for the tow truck to arrive, I thought about all that had happened over the past few weeks—repeated trips to the doctor's office with several of our children, who were very young at the time; the compressor on our refrigerator tearing up and having to be replaced at an expensive price; and now *this*. "Why are so many things going wrong right now?" I asked myself. No sooner had I asked the question than I heard the accusations inside me: "I *have* neglected my quiet time lately, in fact, I didn't even read the Bible this morning. I haven't been praying much either. For that matter, I haven't shared the gospel with an unsaved person in weeks. And then there's that time I lost my temper with the kids earlier this week." On and on the inventory of failures over the past few weeks went through my mind.

I'm not comfortable in admitting that I thought God must be irritated with me because I didn't do the things I imagined He wanted me to do. I only acknowledge it to you because I don't think my attitude was uncommon. In those days I envisioned God to be tense with me much of the time. I knew He loved me; I reasoned that because He is God, that goes with the job description. However, I *felt* that God wasn't always happy with me and sometimes I even thought He was probably exasperated because of my pitiful level of consistency. I've met many believers who are convinced that what they do or don't do determines God's mood toward them at any given moment. They are living in the shackles of legalism by believing that God blesses or curses them based on their behavior. They see God as being fickle, able to have His disposition toward them altered by what they do.

The children of Israel had been anything but consistent in their walk from the time that Moses had first led them out of Egypt and across the Red Sea. Even since entering Canaan, there had been occasional lapses in their faith (see Joshua 7:1; 9:14). However, in spite of God knowing their failures even before Israel knew them, His grace had led Him to give them the land. "So Joshua took the whole land, according to all that the LORD had spoken to Moses, and Joshua gave it for an inheritance to Israel according to their divisions by their tribes. Thus the land had rest from war" (Joshua 11:23). He took the whole land—victory was complete not because of their faithfulness, but God's. The residents of His grace-land always are cognizant of the fact that they have done nothing to earn it, but that complete victory was given to them as a gift.

One Thing Causes God to Be Angry

Some Christians imagine God to be impatient, ready to hurl lightning bolts into their lives every time they make the slightest misstep. That is far from what the Bible teaches about God's attitude toward believers. Generally speaking, the nature of God is that

He is slow to become angry (see Exodus 34:6; Numbers 14:18; Nehemiah 9:17; Psalm 86:15; 103:8; 145:8; Joel 2:13; Jonah 4:2; Nahum 1:3).

What *does* anger God? Using Bible software, I did a search on the word "anger" to discover how many times in the Bible God is revealed as being angry. My research indicated that in Scripture, God is shown to be angry 153 times. I went back and examined the cause for His anger in each of the passages, and in every instance, the cause for God's anger was the same—sin. God *hates* sin. The Bible suggests that there is nothing that angers God other than sin.

> *I* knew God loved me; I reasoned that because He is God, that goes with the job description. However, I felt that He wasn't always happy with me.

God Cannot Be Contained by Time

If sin angers God and we, as Christians, don't live sinless lives, how could one argue that God doesn't become angry with us? After all, we *do* still commit sins. The answer lies in understanding God's transcendent nature over time and the finality of the cross of Jesus Christ. It is true that believers occasionally sin, but our sins have been dealt with *in totality*.

Human beings are time creatures. We experience reality within the parameters of time, which may be described as duration measured by succession. In other words, the occurrence of events in our lives in chronological order produce "time." From the human perspective, all reality appears to be *linear,* having a starting place and a stopping point.

God, on the other hand, is not bound by the confines of time. Time can't contain God. To contain Him, it would have to be greater than Him, and nothing is greater than God. God exists outside the boundaries of time in a place called *eternity.* To attempt to understand eternity, we must look outside the grid lines of time.

A young boy once defined time as "the thing that keeps everything from happening all at once." Not a bad definition! While this earth and everybody on it exist on a path that has often been labeled as a "time line," God sits above the time line of the natural world and sees everything from beginning to end.

In fact, God does more than simply *see* the time line from beginning to end; He has designed it from start to finish. "He has made everything appropriate in its time. He has also set eternity in their [man's] heart, yet so that man will not find out *the work which God has done from the beginning even to the end"* (Ecclesiastes 3:11, emphasis added). God is absolutely sovereign over time. "*I* am God, and there is no one like Me, declaring the end from the beginning" (Isaiah 46:9). Some may be tempted to argue that God didn't write the script for many things that occur in time, but biblical evidence suggests that even Satan himself is nothing more than a two-bit player in the unfolding drama of time and eternity. *God is in charge* of time because He created it and stands above it (see Genesis 1:14-18). He is the Sovereign over every millisecond and each minuscule detail of its history.

God sees into eternity past and into eternity future (as we would understand it). Set right in the middle is the reality we know as time. Existing outside the bounds of time, God sees it all at once. He lives in what many have called "the eternal now." Ray Stedman observes:

We constantly think of heaven as a continuation on a larger and perfect scale of life on earth. Locked into our world of space and time, we find it very difficult to imagine life proceeding on any other terms. But we must remember that time is time and eternity is eternity and never the twain shall meet.[1]

Time and eternity are two totally different categories of experience. While those of us in time experience events successively, the eternal perspective would allow one to see all things contained in time happening *simultaneously.*

They [time and eternity] are not the same, and we must not make them the same. Time means that we are locked into a pattern of chronological sequence which we are helpless to break. For example, all human beings sharing the same room will experience an earthquake together. While there are varying feelings and reactions, everyone will feel the earthquake at the same time. But in eternity events do not follow a sequential pattern. There is no past or future, only the present NOW. Within that NOW, all events happen.[2]

All events happen in the present NOW in eternity. To understand that concept helps make certain Bible verses and biblical concepts much more easily understood. For instance, Enoch saw the second coming of Jesus Christ even though he lived only seven generations beyond Adam. Jude 14-15 says:

Enoch, in the seventh generation from Adam, prophesied, saying, "Behold, the Lord came with many thousands of His holy ones, to execute judgment upon all, and to convict all the ungodly of all their ungodly deeds which they have done in an ungodly way, and of all the harsh things which ungodly sinners have spoken against Him" (emphasis added).

How did Enoch see this event happening when he lived seven generations beyond Adam? It is because he was enabled to see the reality that exists beyond time. Outside the bounds of time, he could look down on time and see Jesus coming again. We, who live *in time*, haven't realized that event yet, but it is a done deal in eternity!

Describing from the eternal perspective what God has done for the believer, Paul writes:

> *For whom He foreknew, He also predestined to become conformed to the image of His Son, that He might be the first-born among many brethren; and whom He predestined, these He also called; and whom He called, these He also justified; and whom He justified, these He also glorified* (Romans 8:29-30).

Paul lists five things that God has already done for those who are His: 1) He foreknew us; 2) He predestined us to be conformed to the image of His Son; 3) He called us; 4) He justified us; 5) He glorified us. Each of these are spoken of in the past tense, as if they have already happened. Why would Paul describe these five acts of God in our lives in the past tense? It is because all five *have already happened* in the eternal realm!

The Cross of Christ Is Sufficient

Every believer has been foreknown, predestined, called, justified, and glorified. Whether or not we feel it or believe it, God's Word says it is true. From the eternal now, God looked down on our lifetime and saw every sin that we would ever commit. He took those sins and placed them onto Jesus Christ, where "He Himself bore our sins in His body on the cross" (1 Peter 2:24). Paul the apostle wrote:

> *When you were dead in your transgressions and the uncircumcision of your flesh, He made you alive together with Him, having forgiven us all our transgressions, having canceled out the certificate of debt consisting of decrees against us, and which was hostile to us; and He has taken it out of the way, having nailed it to the cross* (Colossians 2:13-14).

The certificate of debt mentioned by Paul refers to an invoice used to show the debt an individual owed to a creditor. When he paid the balance on his account, the invoice was marked "Fulfilled," showing that his debt had been completely paid in full. From the vantage point of eternity, God saw every sin you would commit in your lifetime and recorded each one on your own personal certificate of debt. He then took that invoice, showing the balance due from you for your sins (separation from God *in eternity*), and placed your debt onto Jesus Christ. When Jesus discharged the debt for our sin, He cried out, "It is finished!" The Greek word is *tetelestai,* which may also be translated "Fulfilled!"

Author Bill Gillham comments:

> John 19:30 records Jesus' final words on the cross. "…He said, It is finished! And He…gave up His spirit." Do you know what Greek word has been translated "It is finished" here? *Tetelestai!* Oh, my brother, my sister, how profound! How awesome! Preserve this moment—make it a special happening. Get a pen and a piece of paper. Write this heading on the paper: Certificate of Debt. Now write a number across the center of the paper in one-inch script indicating the estimated number of sins

you will have committed in your entire life on earth (as in 10,000,000). Now take a red felt pen and in large block letters write the word TETELESTAI, cutting diagonally across that number from lower left toward upper right. Then at the bottom of the sheet write, "Dictated personally, but signed for Him in His absence," and then sign the name *Jesus*. Fold the letter and place it in an envelope for safekeeping. Anytime someone or the power of sin tries to convince you that you have not been forgiven of *all your sins*, take out that signed certificate of debt and stare at it for a minute or so. Then have a praise and adoration session.[3]

"It can't be true that my future sins are already forgiven!" Patty protested after hearing me teach that *all* of the believer's sins are forgiven. I read her the passage from Colossians 2:13-14. Then I asked her these questions, which I encourage you to answer as you read them:

1. How many of your sins did God know about before you were born? (*All* of them.)

2. How many of them did He record on your certificate of debt? (*All* of them.)

3. How many of your sins did Jesus pay for on the cross? (*All* of them.)

4. How many of them were future at that time? (*All* of them.)

5. How many sins was He referring to when He said, "It is finished"? (*All* of them.)

6. At the time you were saved, how many of your sins did God forgive?

If you didn't answer number six by saying, *"All* of them," I encourage you to ask yourself if you're being intellectually honest. Would it make sense that God would see and note *all* of our sins, that Jesus Christ would bear *all* of them upon Himself, that He would declare from the cross that payment had been made for *all* of them, and then after all that, God would only forgive you for *some* of your sins—namely the ones you had committed up to the point in time at which you were saved? Don't make the mistake of trying to put God in the "time box." He won't fit. He has forgiven you for every sin you will ever commit—past, present, and future. The verse clearly says that He has "forgiven us all our transgressions," not just our past ones.

Every believer has been foreknown, predestined, called, justified, and glorified. Whether we believe it or not, God's Word says it's true.

For many years I believed that in order to stay in a state of forgiveness before God, it was necessary that I ask Him to forgive me for each sin that I committed. This kind of faulty theology raises some serious questions. What happens if I *don't* ask Him to forgive me for a specific sin? Does it remain unforgiven until the day I die? What happens then, when I go into eternity with an unforgiven sin? Nobody can go into heaven with unforgiven sin (imagine being eternally separated from God for calling somebody in another car on the interstate an idiot and forgetting to ask God for forgiveness).

On the other side of the issue, consider this question: Is there *anything* that you know is the right thing to do that you aren't doing? James said, "To the one who knows the right thing to do, and does not do it, it is sin" (James 4:17). Do you see the dilemma? If *all* our sins are not forgiven, then we had better make sure we are living a perfect life, because not only do we have to deal with sins related to doing wrong, but we also have to be worried about the right things we *haven't* done. Keeping track of all that would be enough to give the Christian a nervous breakdown!

Relax—You Are Forgiven!

Christians don't have to worry about sins that might go unforgiven. We can rest in the truth that God has forgiven us for every sin of our lifetime. Remember the *only* thing that causes God to become angry? It is sin. The good news is that your sin was dealt with at the cross. You are forgiven! (see Acts 10:43; 13:38; Ephesians 1:7; 4:32; Colossians 1:14). The cross of Jesus has forever discharged God's anger against you. Christians never need to be fearful of God's anger. "Take courage, My son, your sins are forgiven," Jesus said to the paralytic in Matthew 9:2. John wrote, "I am writing to you, little children, because your sins are forgiven you for His name's sake" (1 John 2:12). When you placed your faith in Jesus Christ at salvation, His eternal response to you was, "Friend, your sins are forgiven you" (Luke 5:20). God won't become angry with us as Christians, because the only thing that causes anger in God has been removed from us by the cross!

God Accepts You, So Accept Yourself

Betsy came to me crying one day. As we began to discuss her problem, she explained that she had committed adultery three times in her life. When she was caught, her husband divorced her. She had been single again for a little over a year. "I know that the Bible says God has forgiven me for all my sins, but I cannot overcome the guilt I feel," she explained. "Every time I date a sincerely good man, I find myself thinking that I can't allow myself to become serious with him because he deserves someone better than me."

Although Betsy knew that God had forgiven her, she had not forgiven herself. Consequently, she was wallowing in the misery of self-condemnation. Many Christians struggle with nagging guilt over their sins. They know intellectually that they have been forgiven, but the truth hasn't reached their emotions. They underestimate the gentle grace of God.

> If Jesus appeared at your dining room table tonight with knowledge of everything you are and are not, total comprehension of your life story and every skeleton hidden in your closet; if He laid out the real state of your present discipleship with the hidden agenda, the mixed motives, and the dark desires buried in your psyche, you would feel His acceptance and forgiveness.[4]

Jesus isn't mad at you! I used to think that He *must* be angry; after all, I would sometimes keep committing the same sin over and over again. Wouldn't my repeated failure eventually wear out His patience? The answer is an emphatic *no!* Remember that God saw *every* sin you would ever commit as He looked at your spot on the time line. He placed all of them into Christ and forgave them all, even the ones you haven't committed yet. Don't believe that your failures can bankrupt God's grace. You can't out-sin the grace of God! (See Romans 5:20.)

Many have asked, "Won't teaching people that God's grace has pardoned all of their sins encourage those same people to commit sins?" Absolutely not. To the contrary, the grace of God teaches Christians to deny ungodliness and to live holy lives (see Titus 2:11). A legalist is afraid of this kind of excessive grace because he has never experienced the freedom to know what sins he might commit if given the chance. And, by the way, the concern that unmeasured grace will lead people to sin isn't new. Paul faced the same concern in his day. In Romans 6:1-3, after having addressed the matter of justification by grace through faith, he poses the question he knows is on everybody's mind:

> What shall we say then? Are we to continue in sin that grace might increase? May it never be! How shall we who died to sin still live in it? Or do you not know that all of us who have been baptized into Christ Jesus have been baptized into His death?

Why won't the believer who knows that all of his sins have been forgiven go out and live a lifestyle of constant sinfulness? It is because he *died* to the sin-life and no longer has the desire for it anymore. This doesn't mean he won't sin. But when he does lapse into sin it will change nothing in his relationship to God.

David Seamands recounts the following story:

> I will always remember a turning point in the spiritual life of one of the young teenagers of our church. He had already made his personal commitment to Christ. He tried hard, but, like most adolescents, was plagued by the ups and downs in his Christian life. So he often came forward to the prayer altar during the invitation time following church services. He had done so once again after a Sunday night service conducted by a visiting evan-gelist. I had prayed with him and now we sat talking at the altar. His face was very sober as he shared with me his determination "to make it this time." Then he asked, "But what if I fail? What happens if I fail?"

I replied, "Steve, I've come to know you pretty well. Probably better than anyone in the church. So I think I can guarantee you one thing—*you will fail. So what?*"

He looked up at me a bit shocked. He had expected me to reassure him, not give him a guarantee of failure. When he didn't reply, I could see he was thinking over the implications of my "So what?"

And then something seemed to dawn on him. It was almost as if the rays from a flashlight had gradually moved across his face. Very slowly he began to smile and to nod his head. "Hmmm...I think I see what you mean. I think I'm catching on," he said. "Of course I'm going to fail; sure, I'll fall. *But that really doesn't make any difference, does it?*" And then the smile lit up his whole face.

Of course, a lot of growth followed, but that was his initial discovery of the way of grace. And his discovery—that with grace, failure doesn't make any difference—changed his life. It was a joy to watch him grow in grace. Later, he became a dispenser of grace as a pastor for eleven years, and now teaches about grace as a professor of systematic theology in a seminary. Are you wondering about my strange reply that I was sure he would fail because I knew him so well? That's because I happen to be his dad![5]

There is no failure in your life that overshadows God's mercy and grace. Just as God gave Israel the land of Canaan and "thus the land rested from war," so it is to be in your own journey into His land of grace. The war with guilt over our sin is done, and we won. We can relax, knowing that "as far as the east is from the west, so far has he removed our transgressions from us" (Psalm 103:12). God has reached from eternity into the time line of your existence and has removed your guilt forever. He will never hold your sins against you again (see Isaiah 38:17; 44:22; Jeremiah 31:34; Romans 8:1).

Robert Capon attests:

> Trust him. And when you have done that, you are living
> the life of grace. No matter what happens to you in the
> course of that trusting—no matter how many waverings
> you may have, no matter how many suspicions that you
> have bought a poke with no pig in it, no matter how
> much heaviness and sadness your lapses, vices, indispo-
> sitions, and bratty whining may cause you—you simply
> believe that Somebody Else, by his death and resurrection,
> has made it all right, and you just say thank you and
> shut up. The whole slop-closet full of mildewed perfor-
> mances (which is all you have to offer) is simply your
> death; it is Jesus who is your life. If he refused to condemn
> you because your works were rotten, he certainly isn't
> going to flunk you because your faith isn't so hot. You can
> fail utterly, therefore, and still live the life of grace. You can
> fold up spiritually, morally, or intellectually and still be
> safe. Because at the very worst, all you can be is dead—
> and for him who is the Resurrection and the Life, that just
> makes you his cup of tea.[6]

*The war with guilt over our sin is done,
and we won. We can relax.*

Think of the worst sin you have ever committed. Do you
have it in mind? Do you remember the specifics of the sin—what
you were thinking and how you were feeling when you committed it? Now think of Jesus Christ hanging on the cross, His
brow, feet, and hands pierced and bleeding. His head hangs in

agony. You are standing at the foot of the cross when He lifts His head and looks you directly in the eyes. He looks deeply into your eyes, and you into His. You feel the love emanating from His gaze, then He speaks: "I *love* you, my child. I know about your worst sin. I know every detail. I know about *all* your sins. That's why I'm here. I forgive you. I *forgive* you; now forgive yourself and let's forget this sin and agree to never mention it again."

If it were possible for a moment to move beyond the restraints of this dimension we call *time* and see the cross from the eternal perspective, *that* is what we would hear Jesus say. All is well. Your sins are forgiven forever. Now, answer this question: Does that realization cause you to want to go out and sin, or does it cause you to want to live a godly lifestyle because of your great love and appreciation for Jesus?

Dear Father,

Thank You that all of my sins have been forgiven. Your grace is so much bigger and generous than I have imagined it to be at times. I accept the truth that You hold nothing against me anymore and that You never become angry with me. I choose now to forgive myself for the same things You have already forgiven through the cross. I love You, Lord, and am overwhelmed with gratitude for Jesus. Allow my lifestyle to express that gratitude from this day forward. Thank You, Father.

G.R.A.C.E. Group Questions

1. What is the one thing that causes God to become angry? Does He become angry with Christians about the sins in their lives? Why or why not?

2. Read Romans 8:29-30. List the five things God has already done for every believer. How is it possible that all of these are spoken of as past events?

3. How many of the Christian's sins have been forgiven? How would you respond to a person who says that the sins we have not yet committed haven't been forgiven?

4. Pretend that you are listening in on a conversation when God is telling someone else about you. What is He saying about your sins?

5. What is the result of failure in our lives as Christians? How does God see our failures? How are we to view our own personal failures? What is the difference between self-condemnation and conviction by the Holy Spirit?

eleven

BECAUSE OF HIS AMAZING GRACE...

Jesus Is Our Only King

IT WAS A WARM OCTOBER AFTERNOON in Hong Kong. I sat with 11 other men around a table. All of us were wiping tears from our eyes. Some of us had our heads buried in our hands and were sobbing. The reason for our tears was because of a song being sung to us by a Chinese Christian named George Chen. Friends from The Bible League[1] had encouraged this stopover on the way to Beijing so that we could meet with George and hear his story.

George began to preach immediately when he became a Christian. Over the next few years, he was arrested numerous times for preaching. As the Cultural Revolution in China intensified, houses were searched and Bibles were seized and burned. Many pastors died and the lives of the rest were in constant jeopardy. However, this didn't stop George from proclaiming the gospel.

He continued to preach until the day came when he was arrested and put into prison. After the iron gate slammed shut behind him, 18 years would pass before he would know freedom again. His notoriety as a pastor didn't serve George well in prison. To make Pastor Chen an example, the communist guards assigned him to work in the prison sewer. Pots filled with human waste from all the prison barracks were emptied into this giant cesspool.

George's job was to spend every day in the cesspool, shoveling the human waste onto wagons, on which it was taken to fields and used as fertilizer. Yet by the divine enablement of the life of Jesus Christ within George, he didn't mind. In fact, he came to enjoy his time in the cesspool. George explained to us:

> In prison, you're never alone. You work beside other prisoners all day, sleep close to them at night and the guards are always watching. This is why I came to enjoy my assignment in the prison cesspool. There I could be alone. The stench of the filth on my clothing and body kept everyone away from me. Nobody wanted to come near me. Not the prisoners, not the guards. Nobody! They all kept their distance.

George continued:

> Since working in the cesspool allowed me to be alone, I was able to pray, lifting up my voice loudly to the Lord. I was able to recite the Scripture verses I had memorized before they took away my Bible. Oh, I would sing! I would sing boldly to the Lord. God's grace sustained me. The living presence and power of the Holy Spirit encouraged and blessed me.

As we sat listening to George's story, one of the men seated at the table asked, "George, what did you sing?"

He answered, "I'll sing it for you now." He closed his eyes, tilted his head toward heaven, opened his hands with palms facing upward, and with a smile on his face, began to sing in Chinese a hymn we all recognized by the melody:

> I come to the garden alone, while the dew is still on the roses; and the voice I hear, falling on my ear, the Son of God discloses. And He walks with me, and He talks with

me, and He tells me I am His own. And the joy we share
as we tarry there, none other has ever known.[2]

As George sang, God's presence in the room became evident
and grown men began to weep. It wasn't difficult to imagine
George in that cesspool, singing praises to God as he shoveled
human excrement. The presence of the indwelling Christ had
turned a cesspool into a garden. George had come to know that
when one has Jesus Christ, he has *everything* he needs.[3]

Christ Is Our Inheritance

After Israel took possession of Canaan, it was time to divide the
property among the people. One by one the tribes of Israel
received the acreage they would have for their new home. Joshua
notified each one about which parcel would be theirs, just as they
had been told by Moses years earlier. "But to the tribe of Levi,
Moses did not give an inheritance; the LORD, the God of Israel, is
their inheritance, as He had promised to them" (Joshua 13:33).

Unlike the other tribes, the Levites were to experience God as
their only inheritance. God had announced His specific purpose
for the tribe of Levi while they were in the wilderness:

> At that time the LORD set apart the tribe of Levi to carry the
> ark of the covenant of the LORD, to stand before the LORD to
> serve Him and to bless in His name until this day. There-
> fore, Levi does not have a portion or inheritance with his
> brothers; the LORD is his inheritance, just as the LORD your
> God spoke to him (Deuteronomy 10:8-9).

The Levites were given *God* as their inheritance. They were to
spend their days ministering in the temple in the very presence of
God, then leave there and go back to their homes in 48 different
cities where they had been instructed to live (see Numbers 35:2-3).

In those cities, the resplendent glory of God would be seen resting upon them as a result of having served continually in His presence. Their lives would be a testament of His goodness and love.

> *The presence of the indwelling Christ had turned a cesspool into a garden.*

All through this book, we have followed the journey of Israel from the time they crossed the Jordan River until they settled in the land of Canaan. This land of grace is a picture of the inheritance every Christian has in Jesus Christ. What the land was to Israel, Jesus is to the believer. After Israel defeated her enemies, the land of Canaan rested from war. Jesus has sat down at the right hand of God because the final victory has been won. He has taken the whole territory, and there is nothing left in the dominion of hell that the cross hasn't overthrown.[4] Jesus Christ is the King of all kings!

Contemporary residents of God's grace-land are those who, by His grace and through faith, have come to know Jesus Christ and who are living out of their identity in Him. We, too, have received *Him* as our inheritance. Paul wrote, "We have obtained an inheritance, having been predestined according to His purpose who works all things after the counsel of His will, to the end that we who were the first to hope in Christ should be to the praise of His glory" (Ephesians 1:11-12). Like the Levites, our lives have been set apart to the praise of His glory. Our inheritance is Jesus Christ, and in Him we have everything we need.

Bible teacher Charles Trumbull wrote that he was once confronted with a rather uncomfortable question asked by a speaker at a convention he attended. The man asked, "Is your kind of Christianity worth sending to the non-Christian world?" He didn't ask, "Is Christianity worth sending?" There is no question about that. But what about *your* kind? Is *that* what the non-Christian world is waiting for, what is needed to revolutionize their lives?[5]

The entirety of authentic Christian living really can be distilled into two main elements. Until these characteristics mark our lives, we will never know the joy of living in grace-land. When these two *do* characterize our lives, we will experience the quality of life that Jesus came to give (see John 10:10).

Experiencing His Life

Our inheritance as believers is Jesus Christ (see Ephesians 1:11,16,18; Colossians 1:12; 3:24). We have the thrilling privilege of resting in the union we have with Him. We are blessed with the opportunity to increasingly explore the depths of His love throughout eternity. Are you *reveling* in the love of Jesus Christ? That's what Christianity is all about—enjoying constant intimacy with Him. Religion shifts our focus off Jesus Christ and places it on ourselves and how well we are or aren't performing. However, that is all unnecessary for the believer.

> The Gospel of grace is the end of *religion,* the final posting of the CLOSED sign on the sweatshop of the human race's perpetual struggle to think well of itself. For that, at bottom, is what religion is: the human species' well-meant but dimwitted attempt to gain approval of its unapprovable condition by doing odd jobs it thinks some important Something will thank it for....Religion,

therefore, is a loser, a strictly fallen activity. It has a failed past and a bankrupt future. There was no religion in Eden, and there won't be any in the New Jerusalem; and in the meantime, Jesus has died and risen to persuade us to knock it off right now. He has said that as far as God is concerned, we're all home free already, and there's not a single religious thing you or I have to do about it. We are, as I said a long while ago, simply invited to believe it, and to cry a little or giggle a lot (or vice versa) as seems appropriate.[6]

Christians don't have to worry about being religious. God has already made us righteous and we can't improve on that. Christianity is not a religion.

You won't learn anything positive about religion from Christianity; and if you look for Christianity in religion, you'll never find it. To be sure Christianity uses the *forms* of religion—and, to be dismally honest, too many of its adherents act as if it were a religion. But it isn't one, and that's that. The church is not in the religion business; it's in the Gospel-proclaiming business. And the Gospel is the Good News that all our fuss and feathers over our relationship with God are unnecessary because God, in the Mystery of the Word who is Jesus, has gone and fixed it up Himself.[7]

In no way is it my intent to cause you to think negatively about the church of Jesus Christ. However, I do hope you are shaken to your spiritual core to see the folly of the empty religious routine many Christians have settled for today. Knowing that they are now on their way to heaven, many have simply settled for dead religious activity from now until they get there. They are going to church every Sunday, giving their money, singing the hymns, reading their Bibles, saying their prayers—doing all the "right" things, *yet they still have a gnawing sense that there must be more to Christianity than what they are experiencing.* They have lost the joy of their relationship to Christ and have settled in with religion for the duration. That is *not* the life that Jesus Christ died to give us!

Our inheritance is Jesus Christ, and in Him we have everything we need.

"It sounds like you are attacking the church with your barrage against religion," Clarence said to me one day.

"No, I am *not* attacking the church. Why does it sound like that to you?" I asked him.

"Because the things you say sound like you are criticizing *my* church," he answered.

"Clarence, I love the church," I assured him. "I was a pastor in local churches for over 20 years. The majority of speaking opportunities I have now are in local churches. What I am attacking is the dead religion found in many local churches."

As our conversation continued, I realized that the church Clarence attended stressed "religious responsibilities" so much more than their relationship to Jesus Christ that he no longer had the ability to know the difference between the two. For him, to do the right things is to be "a good Christian." It saddened me to know that my friend was another casualty of religion. He seemed oblivious to the concept of intimacy with Christ.

"What you're teaching just sounds like mysticism to me," he said. I didn't know what else to say. If the belief that Christians are intended to *experience* personal intimacy with Christ seemed mystical to him, I knew I stood guilty.

Expressing His Life

One by one they approached me, bowing their heads to be touched, to have me pray for them. One woman held out her young son to me, his head covered with oozing sores. I knew what she wanted. I reached out and laid my hand on the child's head and prayed for God to heal him.

It was the first time I had ever been in a leper colony. Tears filled my eyes as I preached to them in Rajasthan, India. "Do you know how *much* Jesus loves you?" I asked the crowd. Heads everywhere bobbed in typical Indian fashion, indicating an affirmative response to my question. As I shared with them that God loves them so much that He left heaven so that they could know Him personally, tears filled the eyes of many. When the service ended I hugged them one at time, while my wife, Melanie, sat in a chair singing "Jesus Loves Me" to a dozen children in the colony who were crawling all over her.

As we left the tent where we had met, the crowd of lepers there pushed in around us, still wanting to be touched, to be hugged, to receive prayer. For the first time in my life I understood what it must have been like for Jesus to be thronged by the multitudes. Melanie and I walked in silence, pondering what we had just seen. Finally I spoke: "If what we just experienced there isn't the ministry of Jesus, I don't know what is."

Loving people. That's what it's all about for the Christian. Whether it's a leper colony in India or an affluent neighborhood in American suburbia, people want to know one thing—that they are loved. Sadly, the modern church often flounders in sharing the love of God with those around us for one simple reason: We don't fully understand how much *we* are loved by Him. It is only when we understand that our lovableness isn't because of our performance but because of Christ in us that we will *feel* the love of God for us. God doesn't love you *in spite of* you. He loves you *because of Jesus* and what He has done *in* you by making you a new creation. You are no longer unlovable! Christians will never be able to effectively express God's love to others until we have embraced His love for us. We must see ourselves as citizens of His grace-land, and that we are dearly loved by Him.

John Eagen said,

> *Define yourself radically as one beloved by God.* God's love for you and his choice of you constitute your worth. Accept that, and let it become the most important thing in your life....The basis of my personal worth is not my possessions, my talents, not esteem of others, reputation...not kudos of appreciation from parents and kids, not applause, and everyone telling you how important you are to the place....I stand anchored now in God before whom I stand naked, this God who tells me, "You are my son, my beloved one." [8]

You can't give away what you don't know you have. Do you know how much Jesus loves *you?* There is nothing a Christian can do to cause God to love him any more or any less than He does at this moment. Your behavior wasn't the catalyst for His love to start with, and has nothing to do with His love for you now. He loved you before you ever believed in Him. He loves you now. He will love you forever. *He loves you.* Rest in that fact and then determine to spend the rest of your life sharing that love with others. Some of the most thrilling moments of your life will be those when Jesus is loving other people through you.

The End of the Journey

Once the land of Canaan had been divided among the tribes of Israel, the people hadn't really finished their journey. They had only begun. The land was all theirs, but they would continue to move forward through the land, driving out the enemy. Faith would be necessary to continue reaping the benefits of this paradise that flowed with milk and honey.

Christians don't have to worry about being religious. God has already made us righteous and we can't improve on that.

Living in the land of God's grace involves understanding who we are in Christ and learning to depend upon Him to be our constant Life-Source. However, that isn't the end of our journey, it's only the beginning. We will spend eternity exploring the depth of our riches in Christ. The things that have had preeminence in our lives in the wilderness of religion will fade to black in this new land. No longer are we ruled by ritualistic efforts to gain God's favor. Rather, Jesus is our only King.

Appropriate your identity in Christ every day, allowing Him to be *through* you who He already is *in* you—Life. With the ears of faith, hear Jesus Christ. Listen as your King speaks to you at this very moment: "I have delivered you from the bondage of your sins.

And I have delivered you from the wilderness of your religious struggles. You are in *My* kingdom now. Rest. Bask in My love and My life. From now on, I will assume complete responsibility for every detail of your existence. You have no more worries now because you have Me and I am all you will ever need. I love you. This is My land; welcome home."

Dear Father,

Thank You! My heart is filled with gratitude as I realize how much You love me. By faith I appropriate my identity in Christ at this moment. No longer will I struggle in the wilderness. I accept Your invitation to live with You forever in Your grace-land. Continually teach me how to live in my new home. You are my King. I love You, Jesus. Amen.

G.R.A.C.E. Group Questions

1. George Chen sang "In the Garden" as the hymn that best reflected his personal testimony while in the Chinese prison camp. What hymn or chorus would you choose to represent your testimony as a Christian? Why?

2. Read John 10:10. Describe the meaning of the abundant life that Jesus Christ said He came to give us. What does this abundant life look like? List three reasons some Christians aren't experiencing the abundant life.

3. Charles Trumbull was disturbed by the question, "Is your kind of Christianity worth sending to the non-Christian world?" Describe the kind of Christianity you were taught as you grew up. Describe the kind of Christianity emphasized in your church now. Describe *your* kind of Christianity.

4. Read 2 Timothy 3:1-5. Discuss verse five. Explain this statement: "Christianity uses the *forms* of religion, but it is not a religion."

5. Identify two ways that you regularly express the life of Jesus in your home, your work, and your church.

A Personal Word

If your life has been influenced by reading *Grace Amazing*, I would be happy to hear from you. The purpose of Grace Walk Ministries is to share the liberating message of the believer's identity in Christ through teaching and preaching, radio, television, books, tapes, and mission outreaches. I would be happy to discuss the opportunity to speak to your church or group. For further information, please feel free to contact me at the address below. I also invite you to visit our Web site at www.gracewalk.org, where you can find information about audiotapes and videotapes on the subject of God's grace.

Dr. Steve McVey
Grace Walk Ministries
P.O. Box 725368
Atlanta, GA 31139-9368
Phone: (800) 472-2311
E-mail: gracewalk@aol.com
Web site: www.gracewalk.org

May God continue to bless you in your own grace walk as you come to "know Him, and the power of His resurrection and the fellowship of His sufferings" (Philippians 3:10).

Notes

Chapter 1: Religion Is Now Poison for Us

1. Romans 8:28 reads, "And we know that God causes all things to work together for good to those who love God, to those who are called according to His purpose." While this verse may be a great comfort to the Christian in distress, there is a proper time and appropriate way to share God's Word with hurting people. An uncompassionate recitation of a verse is not some divine incantation for taking the hurt away from one who grieves. The Waynes of the modern church need more than that.

2. In Matthew 13:38, in the parable of the wheat and the tares, Jesus used the field as a picture of the world. The field in 2 Kings 4:39 could be understood in the same way. It may picture God's pastors going into the world to find the food they serve His people instead of finding it solely in His Word.

3. In Revelation 2:1-4, Jesus speaks to the church of Ephesus about having lost their first love for Him, despite the fact that they were very much involved in religious activity.

4. Michael Yaconelli, *Dangerous Wonder* (Colorado Springs, CO: NavPress, 1998), p. 24.

Chapter 2: God Will Put More on You Than You Can Bear

1. *Nelson's Illustrated Bible Dictionary*, Electronic Database, Copyright © 1986 by Thomas Nelson Publishers.

2. Barbara Taylor as quoted by Michael Yaconelli, *Dangerous Wonder* (Colorado Springs, CO: NavPress, 1998), pp. 118-19.

3. Anthony de Mello as quoted in Brennan Manning, *The Ragamuffin Gospel* (Sisters, OR: Multnomah Books, 1990), p. 16.

Chapter 3: Much of What We Thought We Knew Is Wrong

1. My book *Grace Walk* (Eugene, OR: Harvest House Publishers, 1995) tells the whole story of how God brought me out of religious legalism and into an understanding of what it means to live in grace.

2. Robert Capon, *Between Noon and Three* (Grand Rapids, MI: Wm. B. Eerdmans Publishing Co., 1997), p. 143.

3. Ibid., p. 132.

4. Krister Stendahl, *Paul Among Jews and Gentiles and Other Essays* (Philadelphia, PA: Fortress Press, 1976), p. 7.

5. Charles Kraft, *Christianity with Power: Your Worldview and Your Experience of the Supernatural* (Ann Arbor, MI: Vine Books, 1989), p. 15.

6. Ibid., pp. 15-16.

7. Andrew Murray, *Abide in Christ* (New York, NY: Grosset & Dunlap Publishers), p. 65.

8. F.J. Huegel, *Bone of His Bone* (Grand Rapids, MI: Zondervan Publishing House), pp. 14-15.

Chapter 4: Our Old Sin Nature Is Dead

1. Watchman Nee, *The Normal Christian Life* (Wheaton, IL: Tyndale House Publishers, 1977), p. 35.

2. Andrew Murray, *Abide in Christ* (New York, NY: Grosset & Dunlap Publishers), p. 78.

3. Neil T. Anderson and Mike and Julia Quarles, *Freedom from Addiction* (Ventura, CA: Regal Books, 1996), pp. 66-67.

4. Ibid., pp. 124-25.

Chapter 5: We Don't Work for God Anymore

1. Watchman Nee, *The Normal Christian Life* (Wheaton, IL: Tyndale House Publishers, 1977), pp. 172-73.

2. *Wycliffe Bible Commentary,* Electronic Database, Copyright © 1962 by Moody Press.

Chapter 6: Our Personal Best Will Ruin Us

1. I cite these verses as examples of occasions in Scripture when the word "flesh" refers to behavioral patterns that one expresses when he isn't trusting Christ to empower his actions. Romans 8:9 proves conclusively that the word "flesh" cannot always mean "skin." The verse says, "However, you are not in the flesh but in the Spirit, if indeed the Spirit of God dwells in you." Obviously Paul wouldn't tell these saints that they weren't in human bodies anymore. He meant that they weren't living out of their own self-sufficiency.

2. Charles G. Trumbull, *Victory in Christ* (Fort Washington, PA: Christian Literature Crusade, 1959), p. 23.

3. Andrew Murray, *Abide in Christ* (New York, NY: Grosset & Dunlap Publishers), p. 190.

Chapter 7: God Has Finished Giving

1. Watchman Nee, *The Normal Christian Life* (Wheaton, IL: Tyndale House Publishers, 1977), p. 58.

2. F. J. Huegel, *Bone of His Bone* (Grand Rapids, MI: Zondervan Publishing House), p. 66.

3. Ibid., p. 69.

4. Nee, pp. 64-65.

5. Alan Redpath, *Victorious Christian Living* (Westwood, NJ: Fleming H. Revell Company, 1955), p. 91.

6. Andrew Murray, *Abide in Christ* (New York, NY: Grosset & Dunlap Publishers), p. 65.

Chapter 8: We Are Free from Religious Rules

1. Michael Yaconelli, *Dangerous Wonder* (Colorado Springs, CO: NavPress, 1998), p. 53.

2. "Truth About Standards: Biblical Standard for Christians" (Huntsville, AL: Know the Truth Literature).

3. The list of verses used for their rules are as follows: *Rule #43:* Psalm 1:1; 2 Corinthians 6:14-17; 1 Thessalonians 5:22; Titus 2:12; James 4:4; 1 John 2:15-16. *Rule #44:* Matthew 5:28; 6:13; 1 Corinthians 7:1; Titus 2:12; 1 Peter 2:11; 1 John 2:16. *Rule #45:* Ezekiel 44:20; 1 Corinthians 6:9; 11:3,4,7,14. *Rule #46:* 1 Corinthians 11:3,5-15. *Rule #47:* Proverbs 16:31; 20:29. *Rule #48:* Deuteronomy 22:4; Malachi 3:6; 1 Timothy 2:9; Revelation 21:27. *Rule #49:* Genesis 3:21; Mark 5:15; Romans 12:1; 1 Corinthians 6:20; 1 Timothy 2:9; Revelation 3:18. *Rule #50:* Genesis 35:2-4; Exodus 33:5-6; Isaiah 3:16-23; 1 Timothy 2:9; 1 Peter 3:3-4. *Rule #51:* 2 Kings 9:30; Proverbs 6:24-26; Ezekiel 23:40-48; 1 Timothy 2:9. I note these passages to demonstrate that their religious rules make sense *biblically* to these Christians, despite the fact that they are consistently misinterpreted or taken out of context.

Chapter 9: We Can Do As We Please

1. Alan Redpath, *Victorious Christian Living* (Westwood, NJ: Fleming H. Revell Company, 1955), p. 150.

2. A more complete examination of the tree of the knowledge of good and evil may be found in my book *Grace Rules* (Eugene, OR: Harvest House Publishers, 1998).

3. Ian Thomas, *The Saving Life of Christ / The Mystery of Godliness* (Grand Rapids, MI: Zondervan Publishing House, 1988), p. 181.

4. Lewis Sperry Chafer, *Grace: The Glorious Theme* (Grand Rapids, MI: Zondervan Publishing House, 1992), p. 345.

5. Donald McCullough, *Waking from the American Dream* (Downers Grove, IL: Inter-Varsity Press, 1988), p. 116.

6. Ray C. Stedman, *Authentic Christianity* (Grand Rapids, MI: Discovery House Publishers, 1996), p. 169.

Chapter 10: God Never Becomes Angry with Christians

1. Ray C. Stedman, *Authentic Christianity* (Grand Rapids, MI: Discovery House Publishers, 1996), p. 145.

2. Ibid., pp. 146-47.

3. Bill Gillham, *What God Wishes Christians Knew About Christianity* (Eugene, OR: Harvest House Publishers, 1998), p. 214.

4. Brennan Manning, *The Ragamuffin Gospel* (Sisters, OR: Multnomah Books, 1990), p. 61.

5. David A. Seamands, *Freedom from the Performance Trap* (Wheaton, IL: Victor Books, 1988), pp. 116-17.

6. Robert Capon, *Between Noon and Three* (Grand Rapids, MI: Wm. B. Eerdmans Publishing Co., 1997), pp. 292-93.

Chapter 11: Jesus Is Our Only King

1. The Bible League is a ministry that has had a long and successful track record in placing Bibles into the hands of believers across the world, particularly in places where Bibles are scarce.

2. "In the Garden," words and music by C. Austin Miles. The work is in the public domain.

3. A videotape of George Chen's testimony is available from our ministry. You may contact us at Grace Walk Ministries, P.O. Box 725368, Atlanta, GA 31139-9368, or call 1-800-GRACE-11 to order the tape.

4. Alan Redpath, *Victorious Christian Living* (Westwood, NJ: Fleming H. Revell Company, 1955), p. 162.

5. Charles Trumbull, *Victory in Christ* (Fort Washington, PA: Christian Literature Crusade, 1959), p. 7.

6. Robert Capon, *Between Noon and Three* (Grand Rapids, MI: Wm. B. Eerdmans Publishing, 1997), pp. 282-83.

7. Ibid., p. 284.

8. John Eagen as quoted in Brennan Manning, *Abba's Child* (Colorado Springs, CO: NavPress, 1994), p. 49.

Bibliography

Anderson, Neil. *Walking in the Light*. Nashville, TN: Thomas Nelson, Inc., 1992.

Anderson, Neil, and Mike & Julia Quarles. *Freedom from Addiction*. Ventura, CA: Regal Books, 1996.

Capon, Robert Farrar. *Between Noon and Three*. Grand Rapids, MI: William B. Eerdmans Publishing Company, 1997.

———. *The Astonished Heart*. Grand Rapids, MI: William B. Eerdmans Publishing Company, 1996.

Chambers, Oswald. *Conformed to His Image*. Oswald Chambers' Publication Association Ltd., 1950.

Edman, Raymond V. *They Found the Secret*. Grand Rapids, MI: Zondervan Publishing House, 1960.

Fromke, DeVern. *Unto Full Stature*. Sure Foundation, 1985.

———. *No Other Foundation*, Sure Foundation, 1965.

George, Bob. *Classic Christianity*. Eugene, OR: Harvest House Publishers, 1987.

———. *Growing in Grace*. Eugene, OR: Harvest House Publishers, 1991.

Gillham, Anabel. *The Confident Woman*. Eugene, OR: Harvest House Publishers, 1993.

Gillham, Bill. *Lifetime Guarantee*. Eugene, OR: Harvest House Publishers, 1993.

———. *What God Wishes Christians Knew About Christianity*. Eugene, OR: Harvest House Publishers, 1998.

Gillham, Preston. *Things Only Men Know*. Eugene, OR: Harvest House Publishers, 1999.

Hession, Roy. *The Calvary Road*. Christian Literature Crusade.

Huegel, F. J. *Bone of His Bone*. Grand Rapids, MI: Zondervan Publishing House.

Kraft, Charles. *Christianity with Power*. Ann Arbor, MI: Servant Publications, 1989.

Manning, Brennan. *Abba's Child*. Colorado Springs, CO: NavPress, 1994.

———. *The Ragamuffin Gospel*. Sisters, OR: Multnomah Books, 1990.

Maxwell, L.E. *Born Crucified*. Chicago, IL: Moody Press, 1945.

McVey, Steve. *Grace Walk*. Eugene, OR: Harvest House Publishers, 1995.

———. *Grace Rules*. Eugene, OR: Harvest House Publishers, 1998.

Murray, Andrew. *Abide in Christ*. New York, NY: Grosset & Dunlap Publishers.

———. *The Believer's Secret of Obedience*. Minneapolis, MN: Bethany House Publishers, 1982.

Nee, Watchman. *The Normal Christian Life*. Wheaton, IL: Tyndale House Publishers, 1977.

Needham, David. *Alive for the First Time*. Sisters, OR: Multnomah Press, 1995.

Penn-Lewis, Jessie. *War on the Saints*. Springdale, PA: Whitaker House.

Piper, John. *Desiring God*. Portland, OR: Multnomah Books, 1986.

Redpath, Alan. *Victorious Christian Living.* Westwood, NJ: Fleming H. Revell Company, 1955.

Seamands, David A. *Freedom from the Performance Trap.* Wheaton, IL: Victor Books, 1988.

Stedman, Ray C. *Authentic Christianity.* Grand Rapids, MI: Discovery House Publishers, 1996.

Smith, Hannah Whitall. *The God of All Comfort.* Chicago, IL: Moody Press, 1956.

Stone, Dan, and Greg Smith. *The Rest of the Gospel.* One Press, 2000.

Thomas, Ian. *The Saving Life of Christ / The Mystery of Godliness.* Grand Rapids, MI: Zondervan Publishers, 1988.

Tozer, A.W. *The Pursuit of God.* Christian Publications, Inc., 1982.

Trumbull, Charles G. *Victory in Christ.* Fort Washington, PA: Christian Literature Crusade, 1959.

Trumbull, H. Clay. *The Blood Covenant.* Kirkwood, MO: Impact Books, Inc., 1975.

VanVonderen, Jeff. *Families Where Grace Is in Place.* Minneapolis, MN: Bethany House Publishers, 1992.

Yaconelli, Michael. *Dangerous Wonder.* Colorado Springs, CO: NavPress, 1998.

Books You Can Believe In®
HARVEST HOUSE PUBLISHERS

Experiencing the Romance of God's Amazing Love

A Divine Invitation

Steve McVey

Have you ever wondered...*What exactly does God want from me?*

God's resounding answer is, "I want *you!*"

For years, author Steve McVey's life message has been about the riches of God's grace. And yet he admits, "I feel like Lucy Ricardo on the production line at the candy factory. I can't keep up and I can't swallow anymore...I allowed the mechanics of ministry and 'living a Christian life' to rob me of the exhilarating awareness of the indwelling presence of Christ."

From that awareness, Steve was awakened to an invitation from God... a divine invitation to the kind of intimacy God wants you and every child of His to enjoy.

A Fresh Look at the Spiritual Disciplines

The Godward Gaze

Steve McVey

For all who want to experience a deeper walk with God...

...here is a contemporary look at nine essential spiritual disciplines that have helped Christians in the Godward gaze for centuries. Now they can help you too. You'll learn how to grow in intimacy with God by putting these and other disciplines into practice—

- *Awareness:* seeing His lovely face
- *Quietness:* hearing our Lover's voice
- *Meditation:* bathing in His Word
- *Identification:* living in Union
- *Service:* keeping our eyes wide open

Living in the Kingdom of God Where…

Grace Rules
Steve McVey

Are you "living by the rules"…or are you letting God's grace rule you?

There's a big difference. If you're living *for* God—living by the rules—you'll always be exhausted. You'll feel as if you're not doing enough for Him…and that if you don't "measure up," He'll be displeased with you.

But God never meant for you to live the Christian life that way! His love for you isn't based on how you perform for Him. He sent Christ to set you free from rules. He didn't call you to serve Him in your own feeble power…but to let *His* limitless power flow through you!

What's more, this power is available to you right now. He has provided everything you need for a truly meaningful, joy-filled life here on earth…all because of His marvelous grace.

Find out how to rest in His grace and let Him live through you in *Grace Rules.*

What You've Always Wanted in the Christian Life…

Grace Walk
Steve McVey

Nothing you have ever done, nothing you could ever do, will match the incomparable joy of letting Jesus live His life through you. It is what makes the fire of passion burn so brightly in new believers. And it is what causes the light of contentment to shine in the eyes of mature believers who have learned the secret of the *Grace Walk.*

If you know how to live it, you'll be strengthened by the depth of Steve McVey's insights. If you long for it, you can begin today!

Other Harvest House Reading

Breaking the Bondage of Legalism
Neil T. Anderson, Rich Miller, and Paul Travis

The Bible talks about it. You see others experiencing it—a Christian life that goes beyond fearful, grit-your-teeth obedience…a rich, *joyful* life. Here, in the personal stories of many believers, you'll find encouragement to come home to your Father—the One who longs for your presence and invites you to enter into His deep love. Scriptural insights from the authors will help you understand

- the bondage that results from legalism
- God's path of hope and liberation
- the joyful intimacy you can now experience with God your Father and Jesus your Friend

Classic Christianity
Bob George

Classic Christianity will help you to get back on track in experiencing true abundant living. Life's too short to miss the real thing!

Growing in Grace
Bob George

With a compassionate heart, George helps you discover the joy of grace, find freedom in the midst of struggles, and grasp the abundant life Christ offers.

What God Wishes Christians Knew About Christianity
Bill Gillham

The host of the nationally syndicated radio program *Lifetime Guarantee* takes you on a journey exploring the critical junctures of your life in Christ. Offering biblical insight and real-life examples, Bill Gillham helps you develop a vibrant relationship with the Savior.

Lifetime Guarantee
Bill Gillham

You've tried fixing your marriage, your kids, your job. Suddenly the light dawns. It's not your problems that need fixing, it's your life! The good news is that the Christian is backed by God's lifetime guarantee.